LEGENDS
of the OLD WEST

LEGENDS
of the OLD WEST
Trailblazers, Desperadoes, Wranglers, and Yarn-Spinners

KENT ALEXANDER

FRIEDMAN/FAIRFAX
PUBLISHERS

A FRIEDMAN/FAIRFAX BOOK

Library of Congress Cataloging-in-Publication Data

Alexander, Kent.
   [Heroes of the Wild West]
   Legends of the old west : trailblazers, desperadoes, wranglers, and yarn-
spinners / Kent Alexander.
      p.   cm.
   "Originally published as Heroes of the wild West" -- T.p. verso.
   Includes bibliographical references and index.
   ISBN 1-56799-109-2 (pbk.)
   1. West (U.S.)--Biography.   2. West (U.S.)--History.   I. Title.
F590.5.A43   1994
978'.0099--dc20   94-8758
                                               CIP

Editor: Elizabeth Viscott Sullivan
Art Direction: Devorah Levinrad
Designer: Lynne Yeamans
Photography Editor: Ede Rothaus
Photography Researcher: Emilya Naymark

Originally published as *Heroes of the Wild West*

Typeset by Bookworks Plus
Printed and bound in China by Leefung-Asco Printers Ltd.

Additional Photo Credit: p. 2 Courtesey Museum of New Mexico

For bulk purchases and special sales, please contact:
Friedman/Fairfax Publishers
15 West 26th Street
New York, NY 10010
212/685-6610 FAX 212/685-1307

DEDICATION
★ ★ ★

This book is dedicated to the millions of Native Americans, African-Americans and women who will, hopefully, record their contributions so that tomorrow's history may be more balanced.

ACKNOWLEDGMENTS
★ ★ ★

I would like to thank the staff at the Enoch Pratt Library in Baltimore, Maryland, for their valued assistance during this project. Also, I extend a big hearty thanks to David Schein for his considerable contributions and, lastly, a tip of the old hat to all the scholars whose work I have cited within these pages. The trail to truth is long indeed.

CONTENTS

INTRODUCTION

★ ★ ★

The early settlers often faced uncompromising territory. There were no maps, no graded roads, and access to fertile land, more often than not, could only be gained through hard work. The pioneers would reach the end of a bluff and have to manually lower each wagon to the valley below before the caravan could continue west.

Since the days of Thomas Jefferson, freedom and the spirit of republicanism have served as barometers for the illusive American character, which many see as being shaped by a society that expanded, pulled by a belief in manifest destiny, across what was perceived to be a mostly vacant continent, through the mountain passes of the Alleghenies, over the Great Plains of the Midwest, across the Mississippi River, over the mountains of the West, and out to the Pacific coast.

Through much of the eighteenth century, and most of the nineteenth century as well, the American frontier was populated by the lawless; this was a restless time that overflowed with seemingly boundless energy and was characterized by a brash sense of nationalism. Many early British writers, such as Thomas

Ashe and Basil Hall, who chronicled these early days, believed that the pioneers had sunk to barbarism. But barbarians or not, these early pioneers captured much of the world's attention with their thirst for an unshackled freedom that seemed to be the goal of most who lived on both sides of the Atlantic Ocean.

Facing unforgiving natural elements, these pioneers slowly carved a tremendously large niche into the world's psyche. Interest in the Wild West has not waned over time, either. Countless songs, movies, and fashion items have been created and live on, documenting the period of American history when people trod the dusty cattle trails of Ohio, Kansas, Missouri, and Texas. Today, paperback thrillers and "shoot-'em-up" Western movies glorify the westerner; the men are imbued with an

aura of violence and romance and have become the archetypal frontiersmen, cultural symbols of national importance.

There is a lack of information about women on the range. History has often been described as "the record of the winner" and in this case this phrase rings exceptionally true. Most histories deny the role of any African-American in the establishment of the American West and neglect to record the contributions of the countless women who served as ranch hands. Recently, there has been an overall attempt to document the exploits of the African-American cowboy. However, because women do not appear in any of the available sources, except as the women friends of famous men such as Doc Holliday, or as mass murderers like Kate Bender, or rodeo performers like Annie Oakley, I have used the words *frontiersman* and *cowboy* throughout this text, unless specifically noted. I can only hope that in the future, someone can unearth the invaluable contribution of women in the shaping of the American West.

To continue, though, the character of these frontiersmen has aroused great debate, and contradictions about it abound. One view is that these people were paragons of national virtue—honest, principled, and patriotic. The opposing view is that they were immoral, lazy, and backward drifters. Many times, they were simply defined by what they wore and their ability to ride a horse; perhaps this line from an old popular song, "The Cowboy's Lament," says it best: "I see by your outfit that you are a cowboy." While distinctive clothing and equipment may have set the trailblazers and cowhands apart from others, the wearing of the gear did not necessarily make the man a scout or a cowboy.

On August 15, 1871, the *Topeka Commonwealth* ran this dismal portrait of a cowboy:

The Texas cattle herder is a character, the like of which can be found no where else on earth. Of course, he is unlearned and illiterate, with but few wants and meager ambition. His diet is principally navy plug and whiskey and the occupation dearest to his heart is gambling. His dress consists of a flannel

Above: Annie Oakley performs one of the trick shots that made her an invaluable part of Western lore. Before joining up with Buffalo Bill's Wild West show, she hunted and trapped to feed her family. Left: On a ranch near Cimarron, New Mexico, in 1906, cowboys take a moment from their duties to pose for this photograph. Notice the lengthy ropes used to keep the horses clear of the roped steer.

shirt with a handkerchief encircling his neck, butternut pants and a pair of long boots, in which are always the legs of his pants. His head is covered by a sombrero, which is a Mexican hat with a high crown and a brim of enormous dimensions. He generally wears a revolver on each side of his person, which he will use with as little hesitation on a man as on a wild animal.

If one compares this portrait to the present sanitized image of the cowboy, one can easily see the discrepancies in the descriptions of the two. For today, the cowboy has thrown off the mantle of the uncouth and rowdy horseman, and has saddled up as a national hero, portrayed by movie stars such as Tyrone Power, Gary Cooper, James Stewart, Roy Rogers, Clint Eastwood, and John Wayne, who was also known as the "Duke." The "Duke" probably embodied the concept of the cowboy hero more than any other single man because the characters he played were clean cut, never

Right: Actor Gary Cooper sports an extremely fancy get-up in this publicity shot for one of his countless cowboy movies. It is from stills like this that our culture has grafted the cowboy look. Below: Roy Rogers rode his way into the living rooms and hearts of many Americans, who believed that he emulated the qualities that made the Wild West safe for white settlers. The truth about this sanitized view of the Wild West is only now unraveling.

backed down, never lied, shot straight, punished the guilty, righted wrongs, and were staunchly patriotic.

During the 1980s, the United States experienced a tremendous upsurge in cowboy interest. The reasons for this trend can be traced in large part to former president Ronald Reagan, a former Hollywood actor whose ideology and public speech imagery echoed with cowboy clichés. President Reagan's first acting role was in a 1940 Western, *Santa Fe Trail*. His admitted favorite author is Louis L'Amour, who, during his lifetime, wrote some eighty-eight books filled with idealized cowboy characters. Before entering politics, President Reagan made several Western films (admitting often that he had wished to make more) and, like John Wayne, intertwined his politics with the mythical world

created in B-Westerns. The theme of these movies are typified by a film in which Ronald Reagan appeared in 1953, *Law and Order*; the promotional poster sums up the film and the genre quite well: "His guns were the only law."

This attitude, coupled with America's floundering sense of pride and dignity, has created a latter-day morality play. And, like a morality play, it is subject to conventions of good and bad, black and, almost literally, white. Unfortunately, in the morality play of the Wild West, Native Americans, dark or yellow-skinned individuals, and Mexicans were almost always stereotyped as villains, while white Anglo-Saxon Protestants, thugs who responded to questions with a grunt and a brandished six-shooter, were mostly seen as good and on the side of law and order.

Yet, despite most people's association of the cowboy with America's West, the term *cowboy* actually dates back to Ireland in

Above: John "The Duke" Wayne prepares for action in this movie still from director John Huston's Stage Coach. *The influence exerted by John Wayne's interpretation of a Western hero is still felt today. Notice his "good" white hat. Left: Clint Eastwood, the "Grim Reaper" of the Wild West, had to go to Italy in order to make the type of Western that has become extremely popular today. These Westerns portray a sparsely populated, dirty, and unfriendly vast territory that was often dominated by men of lesser morals than the characters Eastwood played.*

Here is a still life of sorts of one of the most famous events in American Western history, the shoot-out at the OK Corral. It was there that the Earp and Clanton families made a one-minute gun battle stretch far into the future. Notice the "WE" (Wyatt Earp) tooled into the revolver's holster.

A.D. 1000. English satirist Jonathan Swift used the word in 1705 to describe a young man who tends cattle. However, its first modern usage, which appeared in hyphenated form, dates from the 1830s in Texas. Colonel John S. "Rip" Ford used the word *cow-boy* as a description of a Texas border raider who drove off Mexican cattle during that time. Even this early usage already had the slight coloring of someone outside the law.

After the Civil War, westerners used the term *cowboy* to describe ranch hands, not cattle thieves. On October 1, 1883, the Denver *Republican* noted that "It matters not what age, if a man works on a salary and rides after the herd, he is called a 'cowboy.'" In this book, the term *cowboy* is used to describe someone who, for at least part of the year, earns his living as a salaried ranch hand, since cowboys are defined by what they do. Of course, cowboy work is much more than performing a job for a wage; it is a true way of life with a culture all its own.

It is also important to note that most of the Wild West heroes are based on real individuals, although the truth of their lives was often lost in the telling of their stories. Supposedly, Butch Cassidy and Billy the Kid robbed because they were misunderstood and, of course, gave much of their ill-gotten gains to the poor. George Custer, with his large mustache and long, fair hair, was an edgy genius with all the qualities of a Hollywood star.

It follows then that many facts about the lives of these people are unknown. Records were often not kept, particularly as many of these people moved from region to region on a whim. One might say there was a sense of wanderlust that permeated the air.

Many people in this book are known only for what they accomplished not for who their parents were or where they were schooled. Many times, complete years are not accounted for, as is the case with Sam Houston. Available texts merely summarize the non-heroic portions of their lives and describe only the heroic in detail. Unlike the ever-present media in today's world, the news of the Wild West was, more often than not, passed on only to the surrounding people who subsequently passed on only that which they believed to be necessary. News was shared at supper and at church. Occasionally, an item might be printed in a newspaper, but the news was not always the product of an eyewitness. Accounts would vary with each telling; consequently, many stories, such as the shoot-out at the OK Corral, have no basis in fact.

Therefore, many exploits are versions of the truth and are to be believed with the proverbial grain of salt. History is a record, but the recording has often been done around a campfire.

This book is not only an attempt to demystify many of the myths of the Wild West, but is also a look into what might have caused the conflicting vision of America's role models. Hopefully, this text will serve as a guide through those few decades (1865 to 1890, the time of the cattle boom) in America's past that have come to be known as the years of the Golden West and, in the process, highlight the lives of many individuals who not only withstood the harsh environment, but rose above it to become people whose rugged individualism helped to mold the American character into what it has become today. This text will chart a course through the lives of trailblazers such as Lewis and Clark, as well as Daniel Boone; explore the lives of the cavalrymen, soldiers and lawmen, such as George Custer, Doc Holliday, Bat Masterson, and others, like Bill Pickett, who came to be known collectively as cowboys. The latter chapters will unveil the lives of the showmen and -women; the writers and artists that helped to foster this cowboy culture; and the social commentators.

While an honest appraisal of these lives will be undertaken, there will be an emphasis on the deeds that made these people heroes in the hearts and minds of many Americans; deeds that, in fact, continue to fuel much of the United States' image of itself, its popular culture, and its fashions.

Elsewhere in the world, such as Italy, America's cowboy culture has become a subject for movies about violence and yearning. In Japan, young Japanese boys and girls dress up as cowboys and cowgirls and sing the songs of the Wild West in perfect English.

While most Europeans, as well as people of the Third World, are not heavily influenced by America's cowboy culture directly, most, it appears, still enjoy a good Western movie. Today, Wild West shows no longer tour Europe as they did in the late 1800s. In fact, many Americans are reexamining exactly what contributions were made by the men and women who pioneered the West.

No matter what the outcome is, the Wild West is certain to continue to shape at least the American psyche for years to come.

Welcome, then, to *Legends of the Old West.*

Below: Real cowboys taking a moment from their daily duties on a ranch in New Mexico to pose for this early record (c. 1886) of life on the range. Note their simple clothing. Bottom: This painting depicts a cowboy roping a loose steer. Although the feat often seems easy in photographs and on film, great skill is needed to rope and tie cattle.

No. 227 Cowboys in camp

the Ole Southwest

68

Get along little Doggie

CHAPTER 1

TRAIL-BLAZERS

A WASTE AND HOWLING WILDERNESS,
WHERE NONE INHABITED
BUT HELLISH FIENDS, AND BRUTISH MEN
THAT DEVILS WORSHIPPED.

--- MICHAEL WIGGLESWORTH,
GOD'S CONTROVERSY WITH NEW ENGLAND

GO WEST, YOUNG MAN, AND GROW UP WITH THE COUNTRY.

--- HORACE GREELEY, *HINTS TOWARD REFORM*

Without a doubt, Thomas Jefferson was the father (and Lewis and Clark the prodigal sons) of America's westward expansion. From 1784 through 1789, during his five years of diplomatic service in France, Jefferson began to formulate a plan to explore the trans-Mississippi area. After his inauguration as president in 1801, Jefferson, under the guise of a scientific expedition, sent two officers, Captain William Clark and Meriwether Lewis, on a journey through the Missouri Valley, over the Rocky Mountains, and eventually to the mouth of the Columbia River in what was to become, years later, Oregon.

LEWIS AND CLARK
★ ★ ★

Not much is known about Lewis and Clark, whose names are synonymous with the American West and the first days of expansion. History has it that Captain William Clark (1770–1838) was the brother of frontiersman George Rogers Clark and was a military officer when he, along with Meriwether Lewis, co-commanded the overland expedition to the Pacific Ocean between 1804 and 1806. Meriwether Lewis (1774–1809) had been an infantry captain who had served time, until the expedition, as President Thomas Jefferson's private secretary.

What is known about Lewis and Clark is that the two officers left St. Louis in May 1804 at the command of President Jefferson and traveled through the Missouri Valley with three large boats, four sergeants, twenty-two privates, an interpreter, and an African-American, York, who was referred to throughout Clark's journals as "my servant," but who was actually his slave. They carried with them a considerable supply of food, weapons, and goods to trade with Indians. For food, they took fourteen barrels of cornmeal, twenty barrels of flour, seven barrels of salt (which was depleted before their return trip), fifty kegs of pork, and fifty bushels [18 hl] of meal. Worried about Indians, they carried "eighteen tomahawks, fifteen scalping knives, fifteen dozen pewter looking glasses, three pounds [1.5 kg] of beads, six papers of small bells, three dozen tinsel bands, two dozen ear-

Meriwether Lewis (left) and William Clark (right). These two men, along with their guides and companions, turned a seemingly simple scientific expedition into a trek that gave birth to a national policy, manifest destiny.

rings, five hundred brooches, seventy-two rings, three gross of curtain rings to adorn copper-colored fingers or ears."

This trek has few rivals when it comes to a display of courage and determination. The party reached the Pacific coast in the winter of 1805, and Clark reported that at times the "Murchery [mercury] . . . stood at 40 degrees below 0. . . ." He also wrote that the men returned to camp with frostbitten feet and hands.

In September 1806, the Lewis and Clark expedition returned to St. Louis, where they forwarded an account of their travels to President Jefferson. After relating their adventures, the two explorers became national heroes. Meriwether Lewis was made governor of Louisiana in 1807, although two years later, he was mysteriously murdered in a tavern along the notorious Natchez Trace, a pioneer road between Natchez, Mississippi, and Nashville, Tennessee. William Clark assumed the same post in 1813, after a portion of the Louisiana Purchase became the Missouri Territory.

Of course, the scientific expedition that Lewis and Clark conducted was much more than that—it was a preliminary to economic penetration and political domination by the infant United States over Great Britain's hold over the fur trade. When Lewis and Clark wintered in the Mandan Villages, now a part of present-day North Dakota, they discovered that the British were in complete control of the upper Missouri Territory fur trade. After the two explorers returned to President Jefferson, American trappers were encouraged to move into this area to balance out and eventually offset the British economic position, which might have led to British sovereignty over most of the trans-Mississippi. Because of the heroic efforts of these two brave men, President Jefferson's vision of a powerful country that was connected from coast to coast began to evolve. As the road to the West expanded, new dramas did unfold, stories of the way through the wilderness. The subject of many of those tales, both in fact and in fiction, was Daniel Boone.

Charles M. Russell's Captain William Clark of the Lewis and Clark Expedition Meeting with the Indians of the Northwest, *1897, oil on canvas.*

Daniel Boone, who almost single-handedly was responsible for the exploration and the eventual settling of Kentucky, has often appeared as a character in fiction. A rousing portrayal of Boone can be found in James F. Cooper's The Last of the Mohicans.

DANIEL BOONE

★ ★ ★

I had heard that you were happy in the solitude of the mountain-shaded valley, or on the interminable prairies that greet the horizon in the distance, where neither the derision of the proud, the malice of the envious, nor the deceptions of pretended love and friendship, could disturb your peaceful meditation; and from amid the wreck of certain hopes, which I once thought no circumstances could destroy (it is a matter of disappointment in love), I rose with a determined vow to seek such a wilderness, where I would pass a certain number of my days engaging in the pursuits that might be most congenial to my disposition. Already I imagine I experience the happy effects of my resolution. Here the whispers of vituperating foes cannot injure, nor the smiles of those fondly cherished, deceive.

—John B. Jones, *Wild Western Scenes*

This excerpt from *Wild Western Scenes*, published in 1849, is a fictional speech from the book's hero, Glenn, to the prototypical American frontiersman, Daniel Boone, who strongly agrees with the expressed sentiments. Daniel

Boone, in one form or another, has often appeared as a character in literature. One has only to read James Fenimore Cooper's *The Last of the Mohicans* to gain insight to this stalwart pioneer who was almost single-handedly responsible for the exploration and settling of Kentucky.

Daniel Boone was born in 1734 in Pennsylvania. Brought up in North Carolina, the young Boone hunted many times in the neighboring mountains before venturing to the wilderness beyond. In 1769, Boone left North Carolina with a group and, for two years, roamed the bluegrass region of Kentucky. There, the group subsisted on elk, deer, and bison. During this period, Boone and a companion were captured by Indians. Although his companion was killed in captivity, Boone managed to escape and made his way back to North Carolina. But he didn't stay there long.

In 1773, Daniel Boone, his wife and children, and some sixty other people set off for Kentucky, bringing with them their horses, cattle, and meager belongings. The party was attacked by Indians in the Cumberland Mountains, and Boone's eldest son was killed in the fighting; his death prompted the Boone party to turn back across the Powell River and to establish a settlement on the banks of the River Clinch, a tributary of the Tennessee River.

Two years later, in 1775, Boone and thirty men cut through the wilderness in that area, blazing a trail that later came to be known as the Wilderness Trail, and established Boonesborough on a piece of land situated between the Kentucky and Cumberland rivers. Boonesborough consisted of a series of log cabins with an open space for cattle in the center. This was enclosed by a stockade with a two-storied block house in each of the four corners. This settlement was used as an outpost to defeat the many Indians in the Kentucky area, thereby effectively extinguishing any Indian claim to most of Kentucky during the tense period of the American Revolution.

Boone, as founder of the Commonwealth of Kentucky, has been frequently glamorized. The first architect of the Boone legend, John Filson, in his 1784 book, *The Discovery, Settlement and Present State of Kentucke*, depicted Boone as being adamant in his belief that Kentucky would one day be a rich and powerful state. Filson implies that the only reward the celebrated Kentuckian sought, for his years of hardships, was the love and gratitude of his fellow Americans.

In *The Adventures of Daniel Boone*, published by Boone's nephew, Daniel Bryan, in 1813, Boone is described as being chosen by the "Spirit of Enterprise" to bring civilization to the wilderness and to the heathens. An 1851 painting by George C. Bingham entitled *The Emigration of Daniel Boone*, depicts Boone leading a party of settlers, with their wives, children, and livestock, out into a beautiful sunlit wilderness that, as the painting implies, is begging to be put under the plow.

This drawing depicts Daniel Boone as a kindly but slightly aloof father figure. It was often said that as soon as Boone blazed the territory for settlers, he alone would go deeper into the wilderness to avoid human contact.

Alongside this myth was another equally popular one, fueled by a folk cult that developed around 1815 and stressed that the elderly Boone, although able to become one of the richest men in America by amassing "unclaimed" land, preferred instead to remain in the woods, dressed in the clothing of a simple huntsman living free of society's trappings. This image of Boone depicted him as being many years older than he really was. In James Fenimore Cooper's *The Prairie*, the author placed the sixty-five-year-old huntsman at the age of ninety-two.

It is no wonder that America revered this pioneer woodsman who, on one hand, seemed to be the standard-bearer of American civilization and on the other, a child of nature who fled into the woods at the first encroachment of society. After all, Boone was said to have uttered, after moving from Kentucky to Missouri and then seeing Missouri itself become civilized, "I had not been two years at the licks before a damned Yankee came, and settled down within an hundred miles [160 km] of me!" Here was a man who was a pioneer in the truest American sense. He sliced through the wilderness so that others might follow; but once they did, he ran farther into the wilds. Boone personified contradiction.

Therefore, in Daniel Boone, pioneers had a hero who represented the best and the worst of their longings. In Cooper's *The Prairie*, these longings were well described:

This adventurous and venerable patriarch was now seen making his last remove; placing the "endless river" between him and the multitude. his own success had drawn around him, and seeking for the renewal of enjoyments which were rendered worthless in his eyes, when trammelled by the forms of human institutions.

James H. Perkins, writing in an 1846 issue of the *North American Review*, called Boone a white Indian who was led into the wilderness not by the hope of personal gain and wealth, not by the desire to escape the evils of older communities, not by dreams of founding a new commonwealth, but simply by "a love of nature, of perfect freedom, and of the adventurous life in the woods." Perkins believed that Boone would have "pined and died as a nabob in the midst of civilization. He wanted a frontier, and the perils and pleasures of a frontier life, not wealth; and he was happier in his log cabin, with a loin of venison and his ramrod for a spit, than he would have been amid the greatest profusion of modern luxuries."

KIT CARSON

Kit Carson is the best known of America's mountain men, and his expeditions to California in the early 1840s further aroused the country's budding sense of nationalism. Carson has always been depicted with an air of gentility—a quality that previously had never been associated with men of his ilk.

Carson could not have been said to have the following inclinations attributed to typical mountain men by Timothy Flint in his 1830 novel, *The Shoshonee Valley*. Flint wrote that all trappers have "an instinctive fondness for the reckless savage life, alternately indolent and laborious, full and fasting, occupied in hunting,

fighting, feasting, intriguing, and amours, interdicted by no laws, or difficult morals, or any restraints, but the invisible ones of Indian habit and opinion."

Kit Carson was born in 1809 in Kentucky. One year later, his parents moved with him to Missouri, where, at a young age, he was apprenticed to a saddler. After several years of such work, young Carson left to seek a life of adventure in the West. In 1829 he made his headquarters at Taos (in what was later to become the state of New Mexico), seventy miles (112 km) north of Santa Fe. From his base at Taos, Kit Carson often journeyed into

the mountains, trapping or acting as a guide to caravans. Soon, due to his sure and faithful character, he was regularly sought after by anyone with a frontier enterprise.

At this time, the area surrounding Taos belonged to Mexico. Citizens of the United States were not permitted to trap in the territory; however, many groups often led secret forays into the area for the purpose of obtaining furs. It was on one of these secret trapping trips that—due to an Indian attack—Carson and several others crossed a region of near-desert into the area of the Grand Canyon in Colorado, where they were welcomed by local Indians. After receiving provisions, the party set out again and followed the Mojave River up to its source in the mountains of San Gabriel, east

of present-day Los Angeles. From San Gabriel, Carson traveled to the mission of San Fernando, and then crossed over the mountains into the verdant San Joaquin valley.

Carson and his party spent the summer at the basin of the Sacramento River. It was during this time that Carson became very proficient at tracking down stolen horses, often following tracks for a hundred miles (160 km) until finding the mounts. After much adventure, Carson returned to Santa Fe in 1830.

Carson spent the next decade trapping in the Rocky Mountains and the Sierra Nevadas, exploring mountain passes and streams from the Platte and Missouri rivers to the West Coast. During this time he worked with most of the famous mountain men of the era, includ-

Top: Jim Bridger, whom many believe to be the greatest of the Plainsmen, scouts, guides, and trappers. In 1842 Bridger quit trapping and established the Oregon Trail, which opened up the route to the great Pacific Northwest.
Right: Thomas Fitzpatrick, who once employed Kit Carson as a scout. In 1846, Fitzpatrick was appointed Indian agent for the Cheyenne.

ing Tom Fitzpatrick, who was appointed Indian agent for the Cheyenne in 1846, and Jim Bridger, who in 1842 forsook trapping and established the important Oregon Trail.

In 1842 Kit Carson journeyed with a caravan to St. Louis, where he placed his daughter in a school and visited friends and relatives. On the way back, he met Lieutenant John Fremont (who was married to painter Thomas Hart Benton's daughter, Jessie), who hired Carson as a scout and guide at the rate of a hundred dollars per month. This was the beginning of a valuable friendship. Not only did the party, led by Fremont but guided by Carson, get their first sight of Long's Peak in north central Colorado, but they later disproved the report of Major Stephen H. Long, who had gone as far as the peak named after him and returned to the government with the opinion that the area was definitely unfit for those who depended upon agriculture to sustain themselves. Lieutenant Fremont's party believed that it was possible for people to live quite well in the area—which now includes the fertile states of Kansas, Oklahoma, and Nebraska—and said so.

In Carson, Fremont found an invaluable scout and guide, who over a period of many years, assisted in carrying out the wishes of the western expansionists (like Fremont's father-in-law, Thomas Hart Benton) back home. Carson also benefited greatly from this friendship, not only because it offered him employment, but also because the association eventually made him an American hero through Jessie Benton Fremont's later skillful editing of her husband's memoirs. These memoirs soon turned Carson the mountain man into a larger-than-life pioneer in the public eye, much in the same way as Boone's biographers did for him. According to Fremont's book, *Memoirs of My Life*, Carson was:

. . . one of the best of those noble and original characters that have from time to time sprung upon and beyond our frontier, retreating with it to the West, and drawing from association with uncultivated nature, not the rudeness and sensualism of the savage, but genuine simplicity and truthfullness of disposition, and generosity, bravery, and single heartedness to a degree rarely found in society.

The image of Carson as a pure, simple, and extremely noble superman also was helped along by several biographers. DeWitt C. Peters was the first to write about Carson. Peters was an army doctor who was stationed during the 1850s near Carson's home in Taos. Carson dictated an autobiographic narrative to Peters; when the biography was published in 1858, it paved the way for Carson's image as a hero who had acquired all the virtues of a mountain man, but none of the vices. Another biography was written in 1873 by John S.C. Abbott, who based his book on both the Fremont memoirs and Peters's book. However, it is because of Abbott's genteel portrayal of Carson that many believe the mountain man to have never uttered a vulgar phrase or word.

Later, a much different image of Carson appeared—a daredevil horseman who killed grizzly bears and fought hostile Indians. This Carson is the forefather of the thousands of buckskin-wearing, two-gun heroes who later populated the dime novels marketed by men such as Erastus Beadle, and was later the model for those who would fill the television and movie screens. This "other" Kit Carson came into his own in Charles Averitt's book, *Kit Carson, The Prince of the Gold Hunters.* This book has been said to have actually embarrassed Carson. Written in the late 1850s, this book was aimed specifically at a mass audience and included characters made popular by James Fenimore Cooper. Averill portrayed Carson as a massive figure, one who was far more heroic than the upper-class eastern hero who resembled the noble heroes of Cooper's books. In Averill's pulp novel, Carson existed by his prowess and courage alone. Unlike Boone, Carson was not one with nature, but a conquerer of its forces. With Carson, the new western hero became an anarchist, a self-reliant and solitary figure in a hostile world. It was this portrait of the Wild West hero that was to continue into the future.

Lieutenant John Fremont, pictured here with his wife, Jessie, and an unidentified woman to the right. Lieutenant Fremont's scouting party, led by Kit Carson, helped to pave the way for settlement of Kansas, Oklahoma, and Nebraska. Jessie Fremont's biography of her husband helped to create the myth of Kit Carson.

CHAPTER

2

SOLDIERS

AND

CAVALRY

HE LIVES HARD, WORKS HARD, HAS BUT FEW COMFORTS AND FEWER NECESSITIES. HE HAS BUT LITTLE, IF ANY, TASTE FOR READING. HE ENJOYS A COARSE PRACTICAL JOKE OR A SMUTTY STORY; LOVES DANGER BUT ABHORS LABOR OF THE COMMON KIND; NEVER TIRES RIDING, NEVER WANTS TO WALK, NO MATTER HOW SHORT THE DISTANCE HE DESIRES TO GO. HE WOULD RATHER FIGHT WITH PISTOLS THAN PRAY, LOVES TOBACCO, LIQUOR AND WOMEN BETTER THAN ANY OTHER TRINITY. HIS LIFE BORDERS NEARLY UPON THAT OF AN INDIAN. IF HE READS ANYTHING, IT IS IN MOST CASES A BLOOD AND THUNDER STORY OF A SENSATIONAL STYLE. HE ENJOYS HIS PIPE, AND RELISHES A PRACTICAL JOKE ON HIS COMRADES, OR A CORRUPT TALE, WHEREIN ABOUNDS MUCH VULGARITY AND ANIMAL PROPENSITY.

--- JOSEPH G. MCCOY, *CATTLE TRADE OF THE WEST AND SOUTHWEST*

SAM HOUSTON

★ ★ ★

The struggle between the United States and Mexico to possess Texas, although the territory was first claimed by Mexico, was fierce and bloody. Yet the fight for this territory created another hero, Sam Houston, who is to this day considered an archetype of the rugged American individual. Many books and films have documented the life of this courageous man who, in listening only to his own directives, won the battle for Texas and will always be remembered as an architect of American history.

Sam Houston was born in Virginia in 1793, but was raised in Tennessee in Cherokee territory, after being adopted by a Cherokee chief. (Books about Houston gloss over why he was adopted by the Cherokees. One can assume that young Sam's parents died while traveling the plains and that he was alone and in need of a family when he was found by the friendly tribe.) When he reached early adulthood, Houston enlisted in the United States Army, and rose to the rank of lieutenant due to his bravery under fire. In 1818 Houston left the army and studied law. He later became a member of Congress, then governor of Tennessee.

In 1829 Houston returned to live with the Cherokee in the area beyond the Mississippi, where all the eastern Indians had been forced to move. During his stay, Houston learned of the Indians' plaints against the United States government, and when he left the Indians in 1832, he not only petitioned the government on their behalf, but managed to force the removal of several Indian agents on charges of fraud. During these battles, however, Houston made many enemies in Congress and therefore sought to leave the United States again.

The fledgling territory of Texas was Houston's next home. During this time, Mexico was continuing its fight against Texans who were loyal to the United States. Houston knew that the outpost known as the Alamo, which had been unsuccessfully attacked by Mexico prior to his coming to Texas, was soon to be stormed again, as it was the southernmost fort in the area. Although Houston attempted to move Texans out of the Alamo, the leaders at San Antonio would not abandon the post because they thought it to be too valuable to vacate. These men stayed on and insisted on reinforcements, which led to James Bowie, the inventor of the bowie knife, being elected as commander of the garrison, despite the fact that he was soon bedridden with typhoid-pneumonia.

On March 6, 1836, the entire garrison (except for the few noncombatants) at the Alamo was killed by Santa Anna's troops, who

Right: Sam Houston, whom many consider to be an archetype of the rugged American individual. Houston rose from modest roots to become a member of Congress, and later, governor of Tennessee. Below: This 1879 drawing by an unknown artist shows Santa Anna's troops taking the Alamo. During the battle, which took place on March 6, 1836, all but the few noncombatants perished in the attempt to hold the outpost from Mexican aggression.

greatly outnumbered them—several thousand to 182. It is said that the dead, including James Bowie and Colonel Davy Crockett, were piled upon a giant pyre of alternating men and wood, and set ablaze. Later, after the end of the war, the ashes were collected and buried on the grounds of the Alamo.

During this time, however, Sam Houston was away and could not join in the struggle. The leaders of the Texas Republic wanted to chase and do battle with Santa Anna, but Houston resisted their wish to fight. He strongly believed that their business was to run a government instead. This viewpoint created much friction and greatly perturbed the government. In fact, Houston's strong stand is recorded with his often-quoted statement about this decision: "Had I consulted the wishes of all I would have been like the ass between two stacks of hay. Many wished me to go below; others above. I consulted none. I held no council of war. If I erred, the blame is mine."

Houston held his ground. On April 21, he and his small band of Texans, shouting "Remember the Alamo," defeated Santa Anna and the Mexican government at the Battle of San Jacinto, which gave Texas total independence.

In October of the same year, elections for the new government were conducted, and Houston was elected president of the republic. Although a stable government was difficult to establish due to very little income, Houston conducted business with great aplomb, and recalling his days with the Indians, left them alone. Despite Northern reserve about admitting another slave state into the Union, Texas, because of Houston's efforts, was eventually admitted in 1845.

GEORGE ARMSTRONG CUSTER

★ ★ ★

The white man is coming out here so fast that nothing can stop him. The reason for it is, that the whites are a numerous people, and they are spreading out. They require room and cannot help it. Those on one sea in the West wish to communicate with those living on another sea in the East, and that is why we are building these roads, these wagon-roads and railroads, and telegraphs.

— Major General Winfield S. Hancock
in an 1867 address to the Cheyenne

George Armstrong Custer was to many a pale-faced warrior. Brave, handsome, romantic, flamboyant, and genius are all words that have been used to describe this man, who was his own press agent during his brief but dramatic life. To many, especially schoolboys, Custer was a true western hero. He was someone to be adored, and during and after his lifetime, the American public did adore him. The subject of many books and films, Custer typifies the Western hero persona in the minds of many.

George Armstrong Custer, whom the Natives nicknamed "Hard Backsides" for his ability to sit in the saddle for hours on end. Though many did not like him, Custer is said to have never gone unnoticed until Little Big Horn.

Last Stop on Battle Ridge, *a 1976 painting by Gary Zaboly depicting "Custer's Last Stand."*

George Custer was born in New Rumley, Ohio, in 1839. After leaving school, he entered the United States Military Academy, where he graduated at the bottom of his class in 1861. Never one to lag behind long, Custer soon distinguished himself during the Civil War in the First Battle of Bull Run, where Northern troops killed Confederates at a rate of almost two to one. Later, at the age of twenty-five, Custer was appointed major general of the Michigan Volunteer Brigade at Gettysburg, where he once again showed great skill. In 1864, he was appointed to the staff of General Phillip Sheridan and served in the Wilderness and Shenandoah campaigns. It was under Sheridan that Custer hastened the end of the Battle of Appomattox. The flag of truce, forwarded by General Robert E. Lee to Appomattox Court House, was later given to Custer by General Sheridan as a memento.

It was during the Civil War, then, that Custer became one of the army's rising stars. He was the youngest-ever brigadier general in the United States army, and also the youngest-ever major general. There may have been better soldiers than he, but there were none more hardworking and conventional. The Civil War also marked the time when Custer began to adopt his flamboyant and now famous style of dress. According to eyewitness accounts during the surrender of General Lee, Custer wore a white sombrero, a flowing scarf, and gold sleeve adornments; he also had extremely long hair. His rather flashy style made Custer always recognizable to the enemy as well as to his superiors. To put it simply, Custer seldom went unnoticed.

After the Civil War, Custer married and set up house with his wife, Elizabeth, in Monroe, Michigan, where it is said they lived happily.

Although Custer inspired women to love him, his troops had a different opinion of him. It said that Custer tirelessly drove his men and demanded their full enthusiasm. Indians that knew him called him 'Hard Backsides" because he could sit in the saddle for hours.

Custer receiving the flag of Truce appomatox 1865

Top: George Custer receiving the white flag of truce from General Robert E. Lee at Appomattox. The flag was later given to Custer as a memento. Bottom: This 1873 photograph shows a pensive General Custer at work in his office at Fort Lincoln in the Dakota territory.

Top: George Custer (left) and Grand Duke Alexis of Russia (right) posing for the camera. Bottom: Young Sioux Chief Sitting Bull with pipe and headdress. As the settlers arrived West in greater and greater numbers, Native Americans grew hostile and attempted to stem the tide.

Custer rightfully symbolized disdain for the ordinary, for he certainly was not ordinary himself. During active service, Custer often was accompanied by a pack of hounds, which were allowed to sleep in the tent with him. Custer's military uniforms were tailored to his specific designs, and his passion for music is legendary. The Seventh United States Cavalry, Custer's best-known command, never traveled without its band, which played in and out of battle, upon orders from Custer himself, "Garry Owen," an Irish melody.

In 1868, Custer led a raid on Indians who were encamped for the winter in Oklahoma's Wichita Mountains, just short of Fort Cobb. Slipping into the Indian camp at daybreak, Custer completely overwhelmed the Indians, killing Chief Black Kettle, an old foe, in the process. Wisely, Custer immediately returned the Seventh Cavalry to Camp Supply, its army base to the north. Naturally this massacre did not sit well with the remaining Indian settlements in the area, who swore retribution. Nevertheless, this battle did break Indian resistance and paved the way for treaties to move the remaining Indians into yet even a smaller area of Indian Territory (Oklahoma).

In 1875, the Sioux decided to go to war against the white settlers, since they were starving and the Northern Pacific Railroad was encroaching on their domain in western Dakota, where gold was believed to have been discovered by white prospectors. Soon after, during 1875, Custer led an expedition to uncover the gold, complete with journalists to document his discoveries, into the Black Hills of Dakota, where he became known by the Indians as "Long Hair." Custer found that the Black Hills were loaded with gold, as he wrote, "from the grass roots down." Consequently, the situation there soon changed dramatically: The Sioux were living on valuable land, which the United States government quickly offered to purchase from them for the sum of $6 million. The Indian leaders, Sitting Bull and Crazy Horse, turned down the offer, and the stage was set for conflict.

After a series of attacks that seemed to point the way for Indians to leave the reservation, the United States government decided to exert more force. Soon after, Custer rode into his destiny at the Battle of Little Big Horn.

Much has been written about this famous battle, and there are several excellent sources that detail the final hours of George Custer, although there is an ultimate irony to his life. Not one soldier lived to tell the story of what happened on the battlefield. It is also reported that the Indians did not recognize Custer among the hundreds of corpses on the battlefield. Clad in a simple buckskin coat, Custer had cut his hair short before the battle and escaped recognition in his most celebrated hour.

Of course, history has forgiven Custer and now looks upon this final battle as a prime example of that special dash that had carried him throughout his brief but dramatic life. In the end, it can be said that Custer orchestrated his life through a series of climactic events that, in addition to the excitement and heroism their epic nature suggests, led to the tragic end that many call martyrdom.

Frederic Remington, Fight on the Little Big Horn. *Note the contrast between the Indian horde and the solitary figure at the top of the drawing; it is elements like this that helped Remington to create a sense of doom in many of his drawings of the West.*

CHAPTER

3

COWBOYS

AND

DESPERADOES

Oh, I had a ten dollar hoss and a forty dollar saddle,
And I started up the trail just apunchin' Texas cattle.
When I hit the saddle I give a little yell,
The tail cattle broke and the leaders went to hell.
I don't give a damn if they never do stop;
'Cause I'm gonna ride like an eight-day clock.
We rounded up the herd and put 'em on the cars,
And that was the last of the Old Two Bars.
When I got to the boss and tried to draw my roll,
He had me figured out nine dollars in the hole.
I'll sell my outfit as soon as I can
And I wouldn't punch cows for no damned man.

--- A popular version of "The Old Chisholm Trail"

Above: Grim-faced cowboys pose in front of the + L Ranch Headquarters of the Prairie Cattle Company Limited in New Mexico (c.1893).

Contrary to the often romanticized image of the cowboy's casual life on the range, cowboys performed their labor on tightly run ranches. Cowboys worked for ranchers; the ranchers owned the land, paid the cowboys meager wages, and often provided part of the cowboys' equipment. Cowboys lacked the opportunity for upward mobility and often found themselves riding the grub line, that is, moving from ranch to ranch, following seasonal work. Once a cowboy became injured or maimed, he most often found himself unemployed. The work was extremely difficult and was, therefore, young man's work. Some older cowboys were able to stay employed by becoming horse wranglers and cooks. Given this situation, few cowboys could expect to become ranchers themselves, or at least do so legally. Therefore, some men turned to illegal means or donned the badge of a peace officer in order to make a dollar.

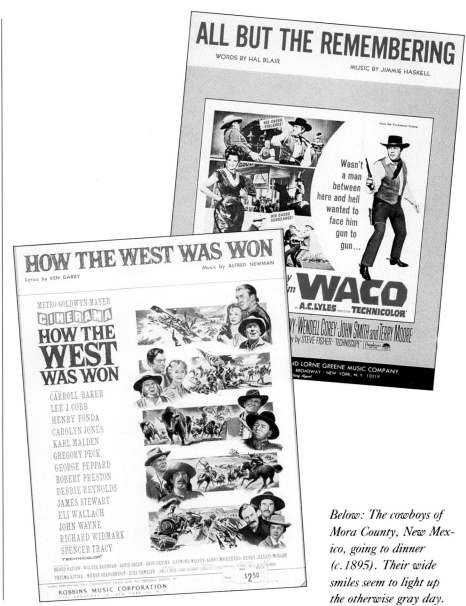

Below: The cowboys of Mora County, New Mexico, going to dinner (c.1895). Their wide smiles seem to light up the otherwise gray day.

JESSE JAMES

★ ★ ★

One of the all-time favorite Western heroes was the United States' version of Robin Hood, Jesse James. This famous outlaw was the leader of one of the most famous bandit groups, the James Gang. He was revered during his lifetime by the poor and downtrodden, and hated by the wealthy—the stuff of storybooks and movies. As with many other Western he- roes, the facts regarding Jesse James' life have been sanitized in order to create a sensational yet palatable hero.

Jesse Woodson James was born in Clay County, Missouri, on September 5, 1847. His (and his older brother Frank's) natural father was a Baptist minister; his mother, Zerelda, had been brought up in a Catholic convent.

Because the wages of tending to sinners did not pay well, Mr. James set out for the California gold mines when Jesse was four years old. Mr. James had lived in California only eighteen days when he died of a fever.

Zerelda remarried, but her second husband soon died as well—from injuries he sustained when he fell from his horse. Zerelda's third marriage was to a Dr. Reuben Samuel, who reported later that he found the young Jesse to be very difficult.

The James-Samuel household was in Missouri, near the Kansas border. Missouri was considered by the people of Kansas to be a wealthy slave state, while the people of Missouri believed Kansas, where prohibition was solidly in place, to be home to nothing but loutish rogues. Therefore, there were often border skirmishes between the two adjoining states, and there was, more often than not, gunplay to stress a point. When the Civil War began in 1861, this only served to aggravate an already bad condition.

Soon after the outbreak of the war, Frank James joined up with a group led by William Clarke Quantrill (a former Maryland schoolteacher), the famous Quantrill's Raiders. (This group was simultaneously claimed by the Confederate army and kept at arm's length. Most historians believe the group operated on their own under the guise of the Confederate army.) Jesse remained at home, as he was only fourteen years old and too young to serve in the military.

The farm of Dr. Samuel was in Northern-occupied territory. In early 1863, when Jesse and the doctor were plowing the field, a patrol of Northern soldiers arrived in search of Frank James. Because they could not obtain the information they desired, they tortured Dr. Samuel, who lost consciousness without divulging the whereabouts of his stepson. When Jesse attempted to assist his stepfather, he was beaten and taken to prison in Liberty, Missouri, although he was later released due to lack of evidence. After Jesse returned to the farm, the soldiers returned and, in an attempt to get information, carried off his mother and his sister, Susan, who after two months of captivity, contracted pneumonia, resulting in the release of both women.

Jesse left the farm. Somehow he found his brother and joined up with Quantrill's Raiders, most of whom were between the ages of seventeen and twenty-five. Although it is said that Quantrill believed Jesse to be too young to join the outfit, two of his lieutenants stood up for Jesse; one of these young men was Cole Younger, a neighbor of the Jameses who would later ride in the James Gang with his brother.

Left: Jesse's older brother Frank, who rode with Quantrill's Raiders. Below: Mrs. Zerelda Samuels, the mother of Frank and Jesse James. She was married three times during her hard life in the Southwest.

Quantrill's group worked as guerrillas for the Confederate army, and this training was important for Jesse, as he and Frank applied this knowledge later. There are countless stories about the escapades of Jesse during his stint with Quantrill and his Raiders. One such story with a humorous bent tells of Jesse, who was supposedly extremely attractive, visiting a brothel often frequented by Northern troops. Jesse managed to convince the madam that he was a girl with an extremely strict upbringing who was seeking a good time. He said that he was not interested in making money, but only in meeting men. Asking the madam when a busy night would be, just to make his time worthwhile, Jesse discovered an evening when the rooms were to be full of Union soldiers. Returning on the night in question, Jesse and the guerrillas entered the brothel; when they left, twelve Union soldiers lay dead. After such a raid, the gang would usually disband and flee to the South to rest, often in Texas. During the first year of the Civil War, some one thousand deaths were attributed to this gang.

After the Civil War ended in 1865, everyone returned home and attempted to rebuild their lives. However, as it was illegal for Southerners to possess firearms at the time, hunting for food became an illegal act. The Northern troops confiscated all horses, so plowing fields was quite difficult, too. These harsh terms, among others, made life for the already crushed Southerner extremely hard. Many Southerners were understandably bitter, since most were destitute and now faced a life of poverty.

The James brothers, however, were busy putting the "skills" they had acquired during their time with Quantrill to use. On February 13, 1866, they staged their first professional bank robbery at the Commercial Bank of Liberty, Missouri. This crime, marred by the accidental murder of a youth with a stray bullet, netted the two brothers $58,000. Several days later, the youth's parents received a note from the James brothers apologizing for the murder. This robbery marked the beginning of a profitable enterprise for Jesse and Frank.

Because Jesse and Frank did not keep a record of their gang or of the train or bank robberies they committed, it is difficult to ascertain which crimes were actually committed by the James Gang (which soon grew to include Cole and Jim Younger and others) and which were simply attributed to the group due to lack of other evidence. Many stories circulated about the gang's propensity to give away money and to help poor Southerners when possible. These popular stories added, no doubt, to Jesse's reputation as a modern-day Robin Hood.

The James Gang was always in transition; its outlaw members changed with regularity. Jesse and Frank were the core of the gang, although Frank wished to give up their life of crime, and Jesse did not.

The James Gang's final bank robbery occurred at Blue Cut, a town just west of Kansas City. Although the take was meager, less than $7,000, the event did mark a significant turning point for the James Gang. There were two bandits that rode with the gang that day, Charlie Ford and his twenty-one-year-old brother, Bob. Bob later turned against Jesse—he murdered him for a $10,000 reward.

On the date of his death, about a month after the Blue Cut robbery, Jesse was at home with his wife Zee (a cousin he had married in 1875, and with whom he had two children)—unarmed. The Fords and several others had been invited over to plan another robbery, but Bob Ford, believing that Jesse had overheard his plotting with law officials to kill the famous outlaw for the reward money, shot Jesse while

Top: William Clarke Quantrill, founder of the infamous Quantrill's Raiders, a Civil War and post–Civil War guerilla group. The James brothers sharpened their outlaw skills with the Raiders. Bottom: Robert Ford, the young man who shot Jesse James to collect a $10,000 reward. He was called a traitor and a coward for his deed.

the latter was attempting to straighten a picture frame. Jesse's tombstone, later erected at his grave site, read:

★ ★ ★

Jesse W. James
Died April 3, 1882
Aged 34 years, 6 months, 28 days
Murdered by a traitor and coward
whose name is not worthy
to appear here.

★ ★ ★

Jesse James lying in state. He was popular when he was alive, but after he died he became a symbol of American restlessness and was seen as an artist whose specialty was robbing banks.

As soon as Jesse died, he became a celebrated outlaw, and myths about him flourished. He soon became a symbol of the insistent restlessness that was typical of the day. While some found expression in song or pioneering, Jesse found his in the robbing of trains and banks.

After Jesse's death, Frank James stopped robbing banks and trains and took work in a Wild West show. He later was employed as a commissionaire for a theater and as a shoe salesman. Frank James died of a heart attack on February 18, 1915.

JESSE JAMES.

WYATT EARP

★ ★ ★

Beautiful, Bibulous Babylon of the Frontier. Her principal business is polygamy . . . her code of morals is the honor of thieves, and decency she knows not. Her virtue is prostitution and her beverage is whiskey. She is a merry two and the only visible support of a great many of her citizens is jocularity. The town is full of prostitutes and every other place is a brothel.
—Robert M. Wright, *Dodge City: The Cowboy Capital and the Great Southwest*

Without a doubt, no city in America has created such a persona for itself as has Dodge City, Kansas. In fact, Dodge City has been eulogized almost as often as the people who populated it in its heyday; one of America's longest-running and most beloved television shows, *Gunsmoke*, starring James Arness as

Marshal Matt Dillon, used the frontier town as its weekly setting. Today, the aging cow town has street names that recall its past, such as Masterson Street and Earp Boulevard. Every year, more than 250,000 tourists visit replicas of Front Street and the Long Branch Saloon. Dodge City was not the original home of Wyatt Earp or Bat Masterson, but it certainly helped to enhance their often fictionalized lives.

Wyatt Berry Stapp Earp, the fourth of six boys, was born on March 19, 1848, in Monmouth, Illinois. He had five brothers: Newton, James, Virgil, Warren, and Morgan.

The Earp family moved to San Bernadino, California, in 1864. Wyatt lived at home until he was twenty-one years old, at which time he went to live with his brother Newton in Lamar, Missouri. Almost nothing of Wyatt's childhood

An artist's interpretation of the famous shootout at the OK Corral, October 26, 1881, showing the wounding of Virgil Earp and the murder of Tom McLaury.

days is known, but it is known that after he moved to Lamar to live with Newton, Wyatt ran against his brother for the position of town marshal and won. One year later, Wyatt married, but only a few months after the wedding, his wife died. His relationship with his in-laws soon soured, and Wyatt turned in his marshal's badge and moved to Kansas.

Wyatt's life is a blur until 1874, except that he was an accomplished cardsharp, until he arrived in Wichita. There, he became a policeman, yet according to reports outside the law, he was arrested and fined for cardsharping on April 5, 1876. Two weeks later, he was fired from his job; a month later, he and his brother James were asked to leave town because they were vagrants.

Over the next couple of years, Wyatt served as assistant marshal of Dodge City and became a deacon of Dodge's Union Church. During this time of seemingly proper behavior, he was earning additional money in the gambling houses.

It was also during this time that Wyatt became close friends with Bat Masterson and James Henry Holliday, who was known to most as "Doc." Because Doc's life is so closely tied with Wyatt's, it is important to take a

moment here to briefly examine the life of this seemingly good-natured and likable man. Records show that Doc Holliday came from Georgia, where he graduated from a dentistry college and thus earned his nickname. Doc contracted tuberculosis during his dentistry education. Because the air out West was drier and more conducive to aiding his condition, he set out for Texas and left his dental instruments behind. He ventured as far west as Dodge City, where he arrived a hardened alcoholic, and settled into the life there with his woman friend, Kate Elder. He soon was befriended by Assistant Marshal Wyatt Earp and Sheriff Bat Masterson.

In 1879, Bat Masterson was voted out of office and decided to move further west. Masterson was accompanied by Holliday and Elder; Wyatt Earp and his new wife, Mattie Blaylock; and Virgil Earp and his wife, Allie. They settled in Tombstone, Arizona, where Wyatt talked himself briefly into the position of

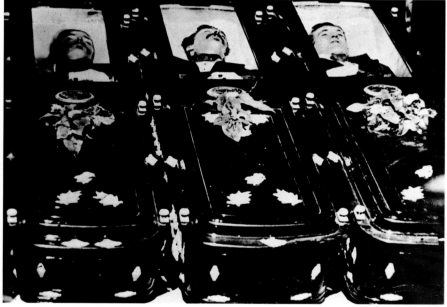

town deputy. For unknown reasons, he was soon relieved of his duties and got a job for a while as a shotgun messenger for Wells Fargo and Company. (Tombstone, named after a prospector who was told before he set out that "the only stone you'll find in these parts will be your own tombstone," was also the location of the famous OK Corral, which was actually a small empty lot where horses were kept.)

Wyatt eventually was hired by the Oriental Saloon to keep the peace among its clientele. It was during this period that Wyatt Earp met up with John Clum, the owner and editor of the *Epitaph*, a local newspaper. Clum eventually became Earp's first press secretary. Clum described Wyatt as "tall, gaunt, [and] intrepid."

After a series of mishaps involving Doc Holliday, Kate Elder (who was forced to leave town after accusing Doc of murdering a stagecoach driver), and several stagecoach robbers, the Earps, now including Morgan, believed that the Clanton family had evidence that would put the Earp family behind bars for the crimes of murder and robbery.

The Clanton family were, on the surface, a respectable farming family from Charleston, Arizona, a mining town about ten miles (16 km) from Tombstone. However, the family conducted many illegal activities, such as cattle and horse rustling. Many people believed the Clantons and the Earps to be two powerful clans who spent a great deal of time plotting each other's demise. With the Clantons possibly holding damaging information against the

Earps, the stage was set for one of the most famous, disputed, and poorly documented gunfights in history, the shoot-out at the OK Corral.

This short gunfight occurred on October 26, 1881; everyone agrees that it lasted no more than one minute. In fact, the only fact that anyone seems to agree on is the length of the fight. Some believe that Virgil was only attempting to preserve his authority as marshal, while others believe that the Earps were only concerned with erasing any evidence that connected them with a stagecoach holdup.

One version says that the three Earps and Doc Holliday walked along the main street and then cut to the back entrance of the OK Corral. They then opened fire on the unsuspecting Clantons. Another version says the Earps approached the corral only to be challenged to fight by the Clantons, who were waiting in ambush. Nevertheless, when it was over, two members of the McLowry gang and Bill Clanton were dead.

Afterward, a Citizen's Safety Committee announced that any further such incidents would be punishable by hanging, and the Earps realized that they were finished as a forceful group. Virgil Earp was shot and permanently disabled as he attempted to leave town. He was never heard from again. Morgan Earp was killed in a saloon battle the following year. Wyatt was not harmed, but the following year he saw Frank Stilwell, a member of the Clanton gang, at the Tombstone station and promptly shot him.

When a warrant was issued for his arrest, Wyatt quickly fled town, left behind his wife, and moved to San Francisco. He later ran saloons in Alaska and then settled in Los Angeles, where he gave an interview to journalist Stuart N. Lake; that interview gave birth to the Wyatt Earp legend, which continues to this day. In January 1929, Earp died and was buried near San Francisco. His tombstone was huge, yet was stolen within days of the funeral.

Two years later, Lake's article, "Wyatt Earp, Frontier Marshal," was published in the *Saturday Evening Post*. Later, when the story was published in book form, it became a national best-seller. Many years later, in the film *My Darling Clementine*, said by many to be the best representation of the OK Corral shoot-out, Wyatt Earp was immortalized by Henry Fonda, and what was left of the truth about Wyatt Earp went up in smoke, leaving behind the character we remember today.

An interesting postscript to this entry is that Doc Holliday left the area after the fight at the OK Corral and remained in the Denver area until he died peacefully in his own bed in August 1886. The following news bit, actually written by Bat Masterson, but credited to Wyatt Earp, appeared in the *San Francisco Examiner* the same month:

Doc was a doctor whom necessity had made a gambler, a gentleman whom disease made a frontier vagabond, a philosopher whom life made a caustic wit, a long lean ash-blond fellow nearly dead with consumption and, at the same time, the most skillful gambler and the nerviest, speediest, deadliest man with a six-gun that I ever knew.

Opposite, top: The famous OK Corral. The gunfight that took place here has been recreated in Westerns and even on Star Trek. Opposite, bottom: The battle at the OK Corral left three casualties, Tom and Frank McLowry and Billy Clanton. This gun battle was the beginning of the end for the Earp brothers in Tombstone, Arizona. Below: Wyatt Earp at eighty. He died in January 1929. His tombstone was stolen days after it was set in place.

BAT MASTERSON

★ ★ ★

Bat Masterson's name has become synonymous with both bravery and nerve. Like other Western heroes, Masterson was made larger than life by books and films; he was also portrayed by Gene Barry on the weekly television series *Bat Masterson*. As a hero of the American frontier, Masterson speaks to the often-romanticized view of gunfighters and shady lawmen.

Almost from the beginning, the Masterson legend was in a constant state of flux. History records that Bartholomew Masterson was born on November 27, 1853, in Quebec, Canada. Only Bat Masterson knew why he claimed to be born in Iroquois County, Illinois, and why as a boy he quickly changed his name to William Barclay Masterson. Certainly neither he nor his family ever explained the discrepancy.

The Masterson family did live in Illinois and later in St. Louis, Missouri, where they homesteaded until May 1870, when they moved to Kansas.

Because schooling in this area of Kansas was almost nonexistent, most young boys spent a great deal of time outdoors, and Bat, like many others of his time, became enamored with guns at an early age. His first gun was an old pre–Civil War rifle, which he used to shoot wild game for the family dinner table. Bat soon mastered the rifle, shotgun, and pistol; he became an excellent marksman, ranked by many to be among the best.

Bat struck out on his own as a teenager and soon migrated to a young Dodge City, where he worked for the Santa Fe Railroad. He soon joined others in hunting buffalo in the forbidden territory of Arkansas (Indian country), where he got into frequent scrapes with the Indians, who considered buffalo hunters to be the worst of enemies.

After many Indian campaigns, Bat returned to Dodge City in 1876 with a mysterious pelvis wound that would plague him his entire life. With his return to city life, Bat discarded his buffalo-hunting clothes and began to wear the outfits he is remembered for to this day: starched shirts, vests, and suits. He began to

carry a series of specially designed nickel-plated pistols, created for him by the Colt Arms Company. During this time he met, and was hired by Assistant Marshal Wyatt Earp, who also befriended him. Masterson's major duty was to ensure peace among the cattle-driving Texans, while extending goodwill toward them, since it was their money that kept the cow town afloat. Because he was still suffering from his pelvic wound, gunplay was painful. Bat would therefore patrol the main street, Front Street, with a silver-handled walking stick. When he would find an altercation, he would crack the offenders on their heads, thereby earning his nickname "Bat."

Opposite: Bat Masterson earned his nickname by hitting offenders over the head with his silver-handled walking stick. Above: Gene Barry, in the weekly television series Bat Masterson, *played a sanitized Bat Masterson. He earned the love of women and men, as well as cut a dashing figure in the Old West of television.*

This group gunfighter shot was taken in 1871 in Dodge City, Kansas. Top row, left to right: W.H. Harris, Luke Short, Bat Masterson. Bottom row, left to right: C. Bassett, Wyatt Earp, McNeal, and Neal Brown.

Bat left Dodge City in 1877 and traveled to South Dakota and then to Nebraska, looking for new adventures. In Nebraska, Bat ran into his old friend Wyatt Earp, who informed him that he was taking the recently offered position of Dodge City marshal. The two men returned to Dodge City together.

In 1879 Bat became sheriff of Ford County, after running for office on the following simple but truthful campaign: "While earnestly seeking the sufferages of the people, I have no pledges to make, since most such are not kept after an election anyhow."

Around 1880, Bat arrived in Tombstone, Arizona, and spent a lot of his time in the Orient Saloon, where he gambled and drank, occasionally assisting his friend, Wyatt Earp, who had moved to the area. In the spring of 1881, Bat returned to Dodge City, but soon moved to New Mexico with his brother, Jim. In 1883, Bat returned again to Dodge City and, while often leaving to conduct business in other towns, he made it his home until 1886, when he moved to Denver, Colorado, and went into the burlesque theater business and earned extra money by gambling. He married Emma Walters, a dance hall girl, in November 1891. He remained married to her until he died thirty years later.

During the early years of his marriage, Bat managed prizefighters. Also at this time, President Theodore Roosevelt offered him the position of United States marshal of Oklahoma, but Bat tersely replied, "I am not the man for the job. Oklahoma is still woolly, and if I were marshal, some youngster would want to try to put me out because of my reputation. I have taken my guns off, and I don't ever want to put them on again."

Bat was later appointed federal marshal for the Southern District of New York. He remained in that job until he accepted the position of sports editor for the New York *Morning Telegraph*. He also wrote articles about gunfights for *Human Life* magazine.

A legend in his own time, Bat Masterson died at his sports desk on October 25, 1921. Hundreds of people mourned his loss and attended his funeral, including Damon Runyon, William S. Hart, and Louella Parsons.

BILLY THE KID

★ ★ ★

No look at the Wild West is complete without an examination of the story of perhaps the first rebel without a cause, Billy the Kid, whose legend is probably closer to that of James Dean than to that of a movie actor such as Gary Cooper, who so often portrayed misunderstood cowboys. Billy the Kid is mostly remembered in film as the young misfit who, on a moonlit night, was killed by Pat Garrett, the sheriff of Lincoln County, New Mexico. Many songwriters, including Bob Dylan, have waxed poetic about the shot Pat Garrett fired that evening—a shot that silenced forever the man history has come to know as Billy the Kid. Despite the fact that he claimed to have murdered twenty-one men in his life of equal years, Billy the Kid is seen as a hero of the Wild West. Part of his mystique, if that is what it is, may derive from the fact that, because he died so young, all that is remembered about him is his boyish face and flamboyant behavior. Legions of historians have combed census records, baptismal registers, and newspapers for clear facts about this baby-faced outlaw, but have yet to tarnish his image.

Billy's life during his earlier years is clouded in controversy and is sketchy at best. Many books written about him state that he was born William Bonney, to William and Catherine Bonney of Brooklyn, New York, on September

17, 1859. Some people believe that his father was unknown and that his mother resided in Manhattan and raised William and his brother Edward alone. Most recently, noted frontier historians, such as Robert M. Utley, believe this information to be incorrect. Since there is no way to discern the truth, this book acquiesces to the most recent historians in the belief that distance might prove the most faithful to the facts. What is inconclusively believed follows.

Above: William H. Bonney, "Billy the Kid," with his trusty rifle. This young misfit has become one of the most famous heroes of the Wild West. Left: Catherine McCarthy, Billy the Kid's mother.

THE FIVE CENT

WIDE AWAKE LIBRARY

Entered according to Act of Congress, in the year 1881, by FRANK TOUSEY, in the office of the Librarian of Congress, at Washington, D. C.

Entered at the Post Office at New York, N. Y., as Second Class Matter.

No. 451. | COMPLETE. | FRANK TOUSEY, PUBLISHER, 20 ROSE STREET, N. Y. | PRICE 5 CENTS. | Vol. I.
NEW YORK, August 29, 1881. | ISSUED EVERY MONDAY.

THE TRUE LIFE OF BILLY THE KID

Billy the Kid was, and still is, a popular subject for cowboy stories. Here an idealized version of the Kid appears on the cover of a five-cent novel of his day.

Billy the Kid, or Henry McCarthy, as Robert M. Utley and others believe his name to have been at birth, was born in the Irish slums of New York City on November 23, 1859, to Michael and Catherine McCarthy.

These historians then cite the 1868 Indianapolis city directory, in which it is recorded that Henry's (Billy was called Henry then) mother, Catherine, told the compilers of that book that she was Michael McCarthy's widow. In 1870, Catherine moved Henry and his younger brother, Joe, to Wichita, Kansas, where, with the assistance of a man whom she later married, William Antrium, she pulled her family out of its impoverished life.

It was in Wichita that Catherine McCarthy and her two sons improved their lives. With the help of William Antrium, she soon acquired property and ran a small but successful laundry business. Years later, after Henry became

known as Billy the Kid, an unnamed Wichita newspaper editor is said to have observed about Billy, that "many of the early settlers remember him as a street gamin in the days of longhorns."

It is believed that because of Catherine's tuberculosis, the family relocated first to Denver, Colorado, and then south to Santa Fe, New Mexico, where on March 1, 1873, Catherine married William Antrium.

The territory of New Mexico was quite different from the streets of New York and Kansas; it was vast, with red, craggy mountains, and deserts. Hispanics, Native Americans, and Anglos all lived there, and the three groups did not always make for a peaceful mix. Because of this and other reasons, violence was the norm in Santa Fe at the time. Here, adventurers from all over the young nation came to seek their fortunes, and the city had a reckless kind of energy that no doubt inspired young Henry McCarthy, who was already known by his stepfather's last name, Antrium, to become an outlaw. Although described by his schoolteacher, Mary Richards, as "a scrawny little fellow with delicate hands and an artistic nature who was always willing to help with the chores around the school house... no more of a problem in school than any other boy growing up in a mining camp," from the start, young Billy was in constant trouble with the law.

On September 16, 1874, Billy's mother died from tuberculosis. This was only nine months after her marriage to Antrium, who, after her death, spent long periods of time away from where he and the two boys boarded, the house of a butcher shop owner, Richard Knight.

During these early years, Henry was remembered for his avid reading of the dime novels of the day and the *Police Gazette*, and a casual drifting toward petty theft. In 1875, at the age of fifteen, Henry and a friend of his, referred to as "Sombrero Jack" in the records, were arrested for stealing a bundle of clothing from a Chinese laundry. According to one Sheriff Whitehill, Henry convinced Whitehill to allow him to run about in the corridor outside his cell. The sheriff left the boy unguarded for thirty minutes and "When we returned, and unlocked the heavy oaken doors of the jail, the 'Kid' was nowhere to be seen." Henry had escaped by shimmying up and out through a chimney.

While certainly not a major incident, this escape marks Billy the Kid's first run-in with the law. More importantly, the escape illustrates the type of brash, resourceful, and daring behavior that would surround the "Kid" during his short life. In addition, this escape also marks a two-year gap in the recording of his life; he literally disappeared from documented history, except for periods when he would surface on charges of horse and saddle theft.

It is believed, due to stories related to historians, that Henry traveled to the western borders of New Mexico, where he worked on ranches and acquired riding and roping skills by punching cattle, tending horses, and performing the many chores necessary to run a horse ranch. It is also generally believed that during this time he learned to use a pistol and rifle. History records that on November 17, 1876, in Globe, New Mexico, a warrant was issued against Henry Antrium for stealing the horse of a cavalry sergeant, Lewis C. Hartman. Henry eluded the law until March 1877, when he was apprehended while eating breakfast in a hotel dining room. He was taken to the army post guardhouse at neighboring Camp Grant, located on the eastern border of Arizona. An hour later, Henry escaped by throwing salt into the eyes of his guard. Soon recaptured and put into shackles, Henry escaped in the middle of the night, "shackles and all," according to the army report. There are two other reports of Henry, now referred to as Henry "the Kid" Antrium, or simply, "Kid," being arrested for the outstanding warrant, only to somehow elude the local authorities.

In July 1877, the Kid returned to the Camp Grant area for unknown reasons. A ranch hand, Gus Gildea, who had worked the area ranches with Henry, described him as being "dressed like a country jake, with store pants on and, instead of boots, he wore shoes. He wore a six-gun stuffed in his trousers." It was at this time that the Kid reached his adult build and began to dress in the mode that he would soon become famous for. Slim, muscular, and wiry, he was said to stand about five foot seven (167.5 cm) and to weigh about 135 pounds (61 kg). He was said to have an oval-shaped face, two protruding front teeth, wavy brown hair, and piercing blue eyes. Henry, according to recent historians, did not wear the outlandish outfits accredited to him in many Westerns, but simple, serviceable clothing, over which he donned a black vest and frock coat. His one fashion quirk was his unadorned large Mexican sombrero. He may have worn the sombrero to

The Finale—the Kid Killed by the Sheriff at Fort Sumner. *This drawing dates back to 1881. Bob Dylan later immortalized this moment in American history with his song "Knocking on Heaven's Door."*

protect himself from the extreme glare of the New Mexico sun. Although described as being reckless, with a hair-trigger temper, many recall him as being generous, open, and possessing a large grin that made those who met him instantly like him. He also could read and write, and was heard to boast of a superior intellect. During this period of time in Arizona, the name "Kid" began to stick, due to his slight build and young age.

In August 1877 Henry got into a fight with a local bully, Windy Cahill, and shot him in the stomach during the tussle. The next day Windy Cahill, the first of the Kid's victims, died. A coroner's jury convened at once and ruled that "Henry Antrium alias 'Kid' is guilty of an unjustifiable and criminal" act. This finding meant that Henry would have been held for the Grand Jury deliberation, but he fled the area and months later resurfaced in the sprawling thirty-thousand-square-acre (12,000-ha²) county of Lincoln, New Mexico, located in the southeastern part of the state. It was here in this mountainous land, dominated by Apaches to the south and small pockets of white settlers to the north, that the Kid soon became a part of the most notorious outlaw gang in the state.

The county seat of Lincoln was a town, also called Lincoln, primarily an adobe village of some four hundred people, mostly Hispanic. The combination of whiskey and guns that dominated the West seemed to be, according to historians, even more prevalent there; intense racial tensions set each group against one another with little restraint from local law enforcement. This was the raw West of legends, and several of New Mexico's most dangerous desperadoes—Jesse Evans, Frank Baker, Bob Martin, George "Buffalo Bill" Spawn, and Ponciano were already a gang when the Kid joined up with them in 1877.

Although called the Evans gang, this group of outlaws was actually a loose coalition whose numbers varied from ten to thirty. They mostly stole cattle and horses and ranged from Silver City, New Mexico, in the southeast, to the Pecos River area in the northwestern part of the state. Often they operated as several bands and referred to themselves as "The Boys." As was often the case with men who lived outside the law, the gang used several aliases. Young

Henry, already using the alias of "Kid," within a matter of weeks was using the name that most would come to know him by, William H. Bonney.

Billy Bonney took up with the Evans gang, with whom he stole horses frequently and, upon occasion, robbed stagecoaches of gold bullion. The Evans gang taught the new recruit how to rob, rustle, and to boisterously enjoy the spoils of plunder. One gang member, whom some believe to be Evans himself, once told a now unidentified reporter for the *Mesilla News* (Mesilla is a town located along the Rio Grande in the southernmost part of New Mexico) "that the public is our oyster, and that having the power, we claim the right to appropriate any property we may take a fancy to."

Another practice of the Evans gang was to sell stolen cattle to local dealers for five dollars a head. These cattle were then resold to the government for fifteen dollars a head to feed troops involved in the various wars constantly being waged against the Apaches, who often were relegated to buying cattle from white ranchers. Many knew that the practice of stealing cattle was going on, but most turned their heads away from the business because contracts were extremely competitive, and there was never any visible link with which to pursue the matter in a court of law. It was in the middle of this range war that Billy Bonney appeared, eager to live up to his reputation as a murderer and outlaw.

It is important here to set the stage for this next important period in Billy's life. The following men are the major players in what became known as the Lincoln County War:

Opposite: Windy Cahill was the first of Billy the Kid's victims. He was shot in the stomach by Billy after an argument and died the next day. Below: This is a drawing of the actual scene at the Maxwell house where Billy the Kid was shot and killed by Sheriff Pat Garrett.

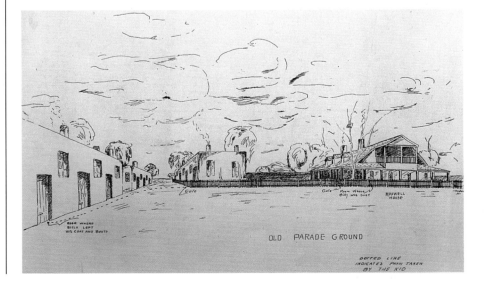

John Chisum: Settled in the area in the 1860s with ten thousand head of longhorns imported from Spain. During the time of Billy's involvement with Evans, Chisum was at the height of his career as the biggest cattle owner in the United States. He held major contracts to supply the U.S. Army as well as the neighboring Indian Reserves. John Chisum is described in history books as large, friendly, and quick tempered. It is also said he could be ruthless when necessary. At his huge ranch, Chisum often would entertain thieves, murderers, statesmen, and businessmen together.

Below: John Chisum was the biggest cattle rancher in the United States at the height of his career. Opposite: John H. Tunstall's grave. During his life, Tunstall was an employer and friend to Billy the Kid.

James A. Brady: Sheriff of Lincoln County. History states that Brady wore a badge, but had no problem taking a bribe.

L. G. Murphy: A retired major of the United States Army. He had run a store in Fort Sumner (some ninety miles [144 km] away). But without expressing cause or reason, he sold it and moved to Lincoln, where he became owner of the only town store and a saloon. Murphy gained government beef contracts by selling meat at extremely low prices. Chisum was absolutely certain Major Murphy was stealing his cattle.

Alexander McSween: Had arrived from the North with a piano and his new wife. McSween was a devout Christian and had obtained an introduction to Murphy upon arrival to Lincoln. Murphy hired McSween as his attorney.

J. H. Tunstall: A twenty-four-year-old Englishman who smoked a pipe and wore knickerbocker suits. He was very wealthy, open, and public spirited. He bought a ranch thirty miles (48 km) outside of Lincoln. He stocked the ranch with horses and cattle, then settled down into what he no doubt thought would be the life of a country gentleman.

★ ★ ★

In the summer of 1877, four rustlers from the Evans gang were caught stealing cattle from John Chisum; Major Murphy then instructed Alexander McSween to work as their lawyer. Now knowing for certain that Murphy was a part of the cattle-rustling ring, the principled McSween refused to represent the Evans gang and was immediately fired. Just as quickly, McSween was hired to work for Chisum. McSween then made another dangerous move. He went into business with Tunstall; they opened a store to sell beef obtained from Chisum, who wished to put Murphy's cattle-rustling out of business if the conviction for the cattle theft did not stick (as was often the case when the arrestee controlled the town and its sheriff). Toward the end of 1877, McSween and Tunstall opened up a bank in Lincoln; this may have been the proverbial straw that broke Murphy's back, for they now had more ready cash available to them than he did.

As this war with Murphy and Sheriff Brady on one side, and Chisum, McSween, and Tun-

stall on the other shaped up, another participant entered the game: Billy Bonney, who had been hired soon after his arrival to work as a cowboy on Tunstall's Feliz Ranch.

According to records, the first shots fired in the Lincoln County War were in 1878. A group of twenty thugs were hired by Sheriff Brady, who, on behalf of Major Murphy, was attempting to collect a rather vague debt that Tunstall owed Murphy. About the time that the posse set out for Tunstall's ranch, Tunstall, his foreman Dick Brewer, and the Kid had set out to hunt wild turkeys. They had separated at one point and, when Tunstall met the posse, he was alone. Who fired the first shot is unknown; however, the outcome is well known. Tunstall and his horse were found dead on the trail between Feliz and Lincoln.

Tunstall's death prompted a series of shooting matches between McSween (Chisum never became directly involved) and Murphy's men. Dick Brewer was appointed as a special constable to hunt down Tunstall's killers. When Brewer was killed during one of the many skirmishes, the Kid took over his duties. At least half of the Kid's income had come from illegal means, but he was smart enough to recognize that with Brady in Murphy's pocket, there was room for someone else to pose behind a badge and reap rewards. By joining Chisum's deputized Regulators, the Kid's reward was simple: He liked to shoot people and the temporary position gave him the opportunity. During this time, Billy often had supper at the Chisum ranch, and Chisum's daughter, Elizabeth, described him like this:

Bad—surely, but surely not all that bad. . . . When he was an enemy, he was an enemy; but when he was a friend, he was a friend. He was brimming over with light-hearted gaiety and good humor. As far as dress was concerned, he always looked as if he had just stepped out of a band-box. In broad-brimmed white hat, dark coat and vest, grey trousers worn over his boots, a grey flannel shirt and black four-in-hand tie, and sometimes—would you believe it?—a flower in his lapel, he was a dashing figure and quite the dandy. I suppose it sounds absurd to speak of such a character as a gentleman, but from beginning to end of our long friendship, he was the pink of politeness . . . .

Of course, Murphy's men would have disagreed with that description. Billy the Kid received credit for gunning down the two men held responsible for the murder of Tunstall, Billy Morton and Frank Baker (both members of the Evans gang); in turn, Sheriff Brady put a $100 bounty on his head. Brady also promised the same sum to anyone who killed any member of McSween's gang (often referred to as the Regulators) or Billy the Kid's gang. Although Brady referred to them separately, the gangs were one and the same. However, the gang seemed to be more under Bonney's command than McSween's, and since McSween, as an attorney, held a position of respectability (and owned the only piano in town), it was easier on the town conscience to ascribe the violence around them to an outlaw like the Kid. For some reason, no one ever connected the gang to Chisum.

The town of Lincoln became so dangerous during 1877–1878 that the courthouse was ordered closed, and the local judge refused to hold court in town. A district judge ruled that McSween and his Regulators were operating outside the law and could be apprehended for murder and lawlessness.

On April 1, 1878, McSween was out of town, attempting to persuade the state governor to see his point of view regarding the judge's ruling. Meanwhile, Sheriff Brady and several of his men were walking down the main street of Lincoln to the courthouse to replace an incorrect notice about when the district court would convene. The Kid and the rest of the Regulators were hiding in McSween and Tunstall's store. When the sheriff and his three cohorts passed by, Billy shot the sheriff, hit him in the arm, and sent his Winchester rifle flying. Soon everyone in the gang opened fire. The sheriff's men ran away. One of the men was caught and murdered outside a local church. Forty-eight-year-old Sheriff Brady was found after the gun battle—with ten bullets inside him. Several eyewitnesses said they saw the Kid leaning over the wounded sheriff, shooting him over and over again with his own gun.

When McSween returned to town, he was furious, correctly believing his attempt to keep the Regulators operating legally to have suf-

fered a setback in the eyes of the townspeople, who had up till then been extremely sympathetic to his plight. McSween's wife, Sue, later told several biographers in 1924 that her husband believed that the crime was:

Billy the Kid's own doing, and was without excuse or palliation [sic]. *McSween had no inkling that such a plot was in the wind. But, if he had known, it was doubtful if he could have prevented it.*

Leaving moral considerations out of the question, the murder was bad diplomacy. It was worse than a crime; it was a blunder. It flouted public opinion and gave the McSween cause a blow from which it never recovered.

After the murder of Sheriff Brady, Billy Bonney left Lincoln and disappeared from sight for the remainder of April. McSween, in a probable attempt to distance himself from the massacre, had indicted the Kid and his cohorts. However, on April 30, the Kid and his wanted Regulators returned to McSween's and took refuge there! In light of everything that had occurred, this situation was insane. Although McSween had sworn out the indictment against the Kid and the guilty party, he was faced with harboring them.

It is written that McSween loved peace more than violence. Since the new town sheriff, John Copeland, was pro-McSween, McSween may have reasoned that he and his wife would be safe and that there would be no battle between the sheriff and the Kid. Of course, the sheriff heard about the Kid's whereabouts and soon attempted to make his arrests. On April 30, a gunfight erupted between factions, and one of the Regulators, Frank McNab, was shot in the back. In light of this, the Kid fled Lincoln again, but occasionally returned to visit Chisum and McSween.

The governor, seeing that the law was not particularly effective, removed Sheriff Copeland from office and appointed George "Dad" Peppin in his place. Still, even with Peppin in

This is the old county courthouse and jail in Lincoln, New Mexico. It was from this facility that Billy the Kid made his famous escape.

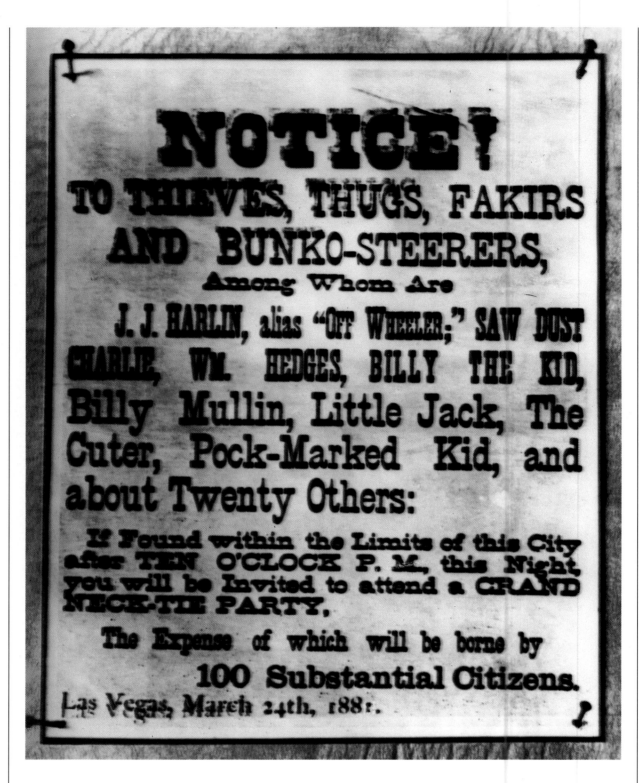

NOTICE!

TO THIEVES, THUGS, FAKIRS AND BUNKO-STEERERS,

Among Whom Are

J. J. HARLIN, alias "Off Wheeler," SAW DUST CHARLIE, WM. HEDGES, BILLY THE KID, Billy Mullin, Little Jack, The Cuter, Pock-Marked Kid, and about Twenty Others:

If Found within the Limits of this City after TEN O'CLOCK P. M., this Night you will be Invited to attend a GRAND NECK-TIE PARTY,

The Expense of which will be borne by

100 Substantial Citizens.

Las Vegas, March 24th, 1881.

office, many minor skirmishes occurred during the spring months of 1878. These battles soon involved Anglo and Hispanic citizens. All of Lincoln seemed to be at war, and by midsummer the town was ready for a true Western bloodbath.

On July 15, a five-day gun battle erupted between Peppin's posse of about forty men and Billy and his Regulators, who numbered about sixty and who were again staying at McSween's house. The fighting was intense, and during the third day, Mrs. McSween, despite protests from her husband, escaped from the house and sought federal help from nearby Fort Stanton.

A Colonel Dudley from Fort Stanton returned with Mrs. McSween, but was more sympathetic to the Peppin forces. While Colonel Dudley was debating with McSween through a series of passed notes, Peppin's posse set fire to the McSween house in order to flush out the party inside.

The fire destroyed the entire house, and flushed out the McSween party. In the process, six men died, including Mr. McSween, who was reported to have passed away holding a Bible instead of a gun. Billy is said to have been the last person to leave the fire; he supposedly exited with both of his six-guns blazing, killing the man who was responsible for McSween's death. In fact, one of McSween's men remarked later that "Billy the Kid was the bravest fellow I ever knew. All through the battle, he was as cool and cheerful as if he were playing a game instead of fighting for his life. When it began to look as if we should be all killed, the other men stood about silent, with long faces, hopeless. But not the Kid. He was lighthearted, gay, smiling all the time."

Opinions such as this gave Billy a modest sense of notoriety in New Mexico. After all, the way the territorial papers saw it, Billy had escaped (with at least three others) after staunchly defending the McSween home.

After the battle, Governor Lew Wallace (the author of *Ben-Hur*) attempted to reason with Billy. He said that if the Kid would surrender and stand trial, he would pardon him. The Kid refused and, after shaking hands with the governor, rode off into the hills. Billy was now nineteen and, with the Lincoln War behind him, was looking for more excitement. He would soon find more than he bargained for.

PAT GARRETT
★ ★ ★

Patrick F. Garrett was born in Alabama on January 5, 1850. In 1856, his family moved to Louisiana, where his father became the owner of two plantations that used slaves. After the Civil War, the Garrett family lost its fortune. Shortly afterward, both parents died of natural causes. At the age of eighteen, after a childhood of prosperity, young Patrick was alone and destitute in a world that was very different from the one he grew up in.

Garrett, like many during that time, moved westward, finding work as a cowboy and a buffalo hunter along the way. In February 1878, he arrived at Fort Sumner, New Mexico, looking for employment after working several seasons as a buffalo-hide hunter. Because of his stature, six feet five (192.5 cm) in his boots and hat, Garrett gained almost instant recognition. He was called "Juan Largo" (Large John) by the Hispanics of the Fort Sumner area, and was said to have been as excellent a dancer as Billy Bonney, who also attended the weekly dances. Pat soon married a young Hispanic woman and, after her untimely death, took another wife. During this time, he had become a saloon bartender. By the age of twenty-eight, Garrett had made and saved enough money to start a restaurant. He was a fairly adept businessman and later bought into a general store and a saloon. He also was well respected by his peers.

By 1880, at thirty, Garrett had gained a reputation as a soft-spoken but resolute and tough man who was not to be crossed. He was noticed by John Chisum, who admired his courage, markmanship, and horsemanship. Chisum recommended to Governor Lew Wallace that Garrett would be the ideal person to serve as sheriff of Lincoln County and to clean out the lawlessness that threatened to hamper his cattle business.

On November 2, 1880, Garrett, after running on a law-and-order platform, was elected sheriff and given a mandate by the people of Lincoln County to live up to his promise. The reigning sheriff, Kimball, promptly appointed Garrett as deputy sheriff for the two months remaining before he formally took office in January. Also, through a clerical error, Pat Garrett was made a deputy U.S. marshal at the same time. Quite by accident, then, Garrett stepped into a situation with Billy the Kid that would make them both legends.

Some accounts say that Billy the Kid and Pat Garrett were very close, that they often drank, played cards, and went to dances together. There are those that say they even went so far as to loan each other money. After all, in the days of the Wild West an outlaw was tolerated in any given community as long as he behaved himself, and except for his doings outside of town, Billy did behave himself.

During this time, though, the Kid was not only rustling cattle from John Chisum, but according to the U.S. Treasury Department, was working with a counterfeiting ring in the Fort Sumner area. It was because of this activity that the federal government wanted Billy Bonney stopped. Billy now had two enemies: the federal government, and a man who once had been his friend, John Chisum.

Once competition like Murphy was out of the way (Murphy went bankrupt during the Lincoln War), Chisum had looked to the future—and the future was the cattle business. Lincoln County was the only region in the area

Pat Garrett. Many said that Garrett and Billy the Kid were once friends.

that was not thriving due to the massive influx of people. Chisum soon saw that his ex-employee, Billy Bonney, was the main reason for this. Bonney was now the highest-profile figure in the area who was stealing cattle and horses. These activities made many that were now coming to the West from the already crowded East extremely nervous; therefore, they avoided Lincoln County.

The government and Chisum turned to Pat Garrett for help. Garrett had no real qualifications to hunt down the Kid except for his expert marksmanship and his knowledge of his friend's habits. As is often said, a friend makes an ideal enemy, since he knows how the other will react in certain circumstances, particularly when weapons are involved.

In late November of 1880 Billy was celebrating with four henchmen in the nearby town of White Oaks. They had stolen four stallions, four geldings, four mares, and four fillies, valued in all at $1,600. The men were hiding out at "Whiskey Jim" Greathouse's ranch, a way station on the road between Las Vegas and White Oaks, and a place where Billy and his friends liked to hold and dispose of their stolen horses. This time, however, Billy and his men were followed to the ranch by a posse who quickly surrounded the building. The cook's child was outside gathering wood and was given a note demanding Billy's surrender. The note was returned to the posse with the Kid's typical reply, "Go to hell," written across the opposite side.

A blacksmith in the posse, one Carlyle, who was on familiar terms with the Kid, went into the ranch house to ask Billy to surrender before any shooting broke out. As a gesture of good faith, Greathouse went outside with the posse. Apparently, while Carlyle was inside arguing (or drinking, depending which version of the tale you adhere to) with the outlaws, one of the men in the posse accidentally discharged his rifle. Perhaps Carlyle believed a fellow posse member had just shot Greathouse, for he attempted to jump outside through a nearby window. It is said that when Carlyle landed, he had three bullets inside him, at least one belonging to the Kid.

The posse then fired upon the house for hours, but with the winter cold setting in, they

Another photograph of Pat Garrett. Garrett was hired by the government to find and kill Billy the Kid.

grew cold, gave up the siege, and returned to White Oaks. The next day, a posse of lawmen returned and burned the ranch to the ground in an attempt to ensure that Greathouse would never again harbor outlaws like Billy and his friends. Before the posse arrived in the morning, Billy and his men already had moved off toward Fort Sumner, where Billy felt safe.

Pat Garrett was hired to track Billy down and bring him to justice. In December, Garrett learned that Billy and his friends planned to attend a dance at Fort Sumner. He set up an ambush. One of the Kid's men, Tom O'Folliard, was riding ahead of the group and was killed, giving the others enough time to escape to an old, run-down farmhouse in nearby Stinking Springs. When the posse found the Kid and his men, one of the gang members, Charlie Bowdre, was outside with a sack of oats. Bowdre was asked to surrender, but he went for his gun and was shot where he stood.

Pat Garrett as he appeared later in his life. It is strange that it is well known that he shot and killed the legendary Billy the Kid, but his own time and place of death remain a mystery.

Bonney and two men, Billy Wilson and Dave Rudabaugh, decided to surrender to Garrett and his posse.

Billy the Kid was tried in the nearest town, Mesilla, the same place where only a few years before Billy had been nicknamed the "Kid" by local cowboys. There he was arraigned on two charges, for the murders of a military officer on a nearby Indian reservation and Sheriff Brady. Billy beat the first charge, since there were no eyewitnesses to testify against him. The second charge, however, was the one that stuck. For this, there were three eyewitnesses, one of which was "Dad" Peppin. The jury returned a verdict of guilty and sentenced William H. Bonney to death by hanging on May 13, 1881.

While in jail awaiting his execution, the Kid was kept in a separate room from the others, and was guarded by two men, Bob Olinger and James Bell. It was here that Pat Garrett spoke with the Kid. Garrett later said, "He [Billy] expressed no enmity towards me, but evinced respect and confidence in me . . . acknowledging that I had only done my duty, without malice, and had treated him with marked leniency and kindness." Garrett also said, "I knew the desperate character of the man. That he was daring and unscrupulous, and that he would sacrifice the lives of a hundred men who stood between him and liberty." Garrett, after cautioning the two men about keeping a close watch on Billy, decided to go to White Oaks to collect taxes.

On April 28, Billy made his move. There are several accounts of this story, and the following is the one recently accepted by leading historians. It is said that Billy conned Bell, a man he liked, to walk him alone to the privy behind the courthouse. Returning, Bell fell behind; when Billy reached the top of the interior staircase that led back to the jail, he managed to slip his hand from the cuffs he was wearing (his hands were said to be smaller than his wrists), smashed the guard twice on his head, and grabbed Bell's gun. Bell worked himself loose from Billy's grip and started down the stairs, but Billy then shot him. Bell tumbled down the stairs, dead.

Quickly grabbing some guns and ammunition, Billy returned to his room and took up a position near his window, waiting for the return of Bob Olinger, whom he hated. Billy's own words tell the story: "I stuck the gun through the window and said, 'Look up, old boy, and see what you get.' Bob looked up, and I let him have both barrels right in the face and breast." The Kid then went to another window and called out to a man named Gauss, who had been with Olinger when he was shot. Billy ordered Gauss to throw up a pickax to him; perhaps due to fear and friendship, Gauss did as he was told. Again following Billy's orders, Gauss saddled up a horse. Billy used the pickax to sever the chains that connected his leg shackles, and as he rode out of town a crowd gathered. An unnamed observer remarked, "The balance of the population, whether friends or enemies of the Kid, manifested no disposition to molest him."

It was reported from other observers that Billy said that he had not wanted to kill Bell, but he felt he had no choice, since Bell had decided to run for it. He is said to have shattered Olinger's shotgun over the porch railing of the jail and, tossing the broken pieces toward the dead man, quipped, "Here is your gun, God damn you. You won't follow me with it any longer."

Of course, the news of the Kid's desperate escape electrified the entire territory. This breakout, bold and intelligent in execution, cemented his reputation as a desperado. The *Las Vegas Gazette* called him "the most dreaded desperado" and "New Mexico's premier desperado." The *Las Vegas Optic* called him a "young demon" and a "terror and disgrace of New Mexico," a "flagrant violator of every law," and a "murderer from infancy."

The news of Billy's escape steeled the nerves of Pat Garrett, and by the end of May, Garrett began to hunt for Billy. By the summer, the hunt had gone cold. Garrett, like most others, assumed the Kid had escaped to Mexico, since he spoke fluent Spanish and was well liked by many of the Hispanics in the area.

However, for some unknown reason, the Kid surfaced once again in the Fort Sumner area. Many speculate that he had a woman friend there. It is certain that he did have many friends, women and men, in the area; however, the exact reason why Billy returned followed him to his grave.

Even with Billy so near, Pat Garrett might not have found him if it weren't for a drunkard named George Graham. Graham had been sleeping off a drunk in a livery stable at White Oaks when two men, probably the owners, West and Dedrick, came in. Not seeing Graham, they spoke together about Billy, who was hiding out with them near Fort Sumner, and had been to White Oaks twice. Graham, for the price of one dollar—or the price of four whiskies at the time—sold the information to Pat Garrett.

Garrett assembled a small posse and went in search of Billy. He found him on July 14, 1881. Perhaps it was an accident or fate that made Pat Garrett and two deputies, John Poe and Tip McKinney, arrive at the ranch house of Pete Maxwell on the same night that Billy did.

Left to right: Pat Garrett, Jim Brent, and John Poe.

Hollywood actor Buster Crabbe, who portrayed many cowboys during his film career, once played Billy the Kid, as did Robert Taylor, Mack Brown, Kris Kristofferson, Marlon Brando, and Paul Newman.

Garrett and his posse had visited Billy's supposed hideout and had found nothing. They were tired and were going to ask Pete Maxwell if he had heard any news of the Kid; if not, they were going to give up the search.

Billy had, unknown to Maxwell, arrived within the same hour. He was hungry and a servant had said she would cook him a steak if he would go and cut the meat himself. As the story goes, Poe and McKinney waited on the porch while Garrett went inside to visit with his ex-employer. It was eleven o'clock and still extremely warm. Around midnight, a smallish figure left an adjoining building and walked across the moonlit yard to the front door of the house. He carried a six-gun and a large knife in his belt. When he saw McKinney and Poe sitting on the porch, he slowed his step. Poe said, "I'm not going to hurt you," thinking the young man to be a sheep herdsman.

Inside, in the darkness of the room, Garrett sat in a chair and Maxwell stayed in his bed. The Kid entered the room and, in Spanish, asked Maxwell who the men outside were. Garrett, during this time, drew his gun from his holster, and the Kid, seeing the movement, turned and asked, "Who's that?" Garrett didn't answer and fired two shots. The first shot went through the Kid's heart and the second went wide: a legend was dead at twenty-one.

This image made Billy the Kid irresistible to the public. To this date, there are more than forty films about his short, tragic life. Such actors as Mack Brown, Buster Crabbe, Robert Taylor, Paul Newman, Kris Kristofferson, and Marlon Brando have fleshed out his life on the silver screen. Books, films, and articles continue to keep alive the myth of this giant of folk legend. Perhaps what society has made of Billy the Kid, alias William Bonney, alias Henry Antrium, says more about society than it says about this young man whom John Chisum called "Happy-go-lucky all the time." At the very least, his idealized life presents an American ambivalence toward violence and corruption amid a simultaneous drive for power and wealth. For these reasons, Billy's legacy still thrives today.

Left: Actor Robert Taylor, wearing a black hat and with six-shooter drawn, appears to be a formidable adversary. Below: Paul Newman, with his stunning blue eyes, was a natural to play Billy the Kid as a romantic and misunderstood gunslinger.

On the afternoon of July 15, at Fort Sumner, the Kid was given his final respects and was laid to rest next to his old friends from the Lincoln County War days, Charlie Bowdre and Tom O'Folliard. It is reported that the majority of the Hispanic community showed up for his funeral, since they claimed him as one of theirs. For the next twenty years of his life, Pat Garrett enjoyed the fame that came with the title of "The Man That Shot Billy the Kid." But the exact date of Garrett's death is not recorded in books about this famous chapter in Western history.

Garrett's deed did take on a larger-than-life aura, as the Kid's reputation blossomed after his dramatic death. The pulp press of the era had a field day. Within one year, five so-called biographies of Billy the Kid appeared in dime-novel format, including such titles as *The Daredevil Deeds of Billy the Kid* and *Billy the "Kid" and His Girl.*

Billy's legend thrived and in the 1950s he became a "social bandit," much like Robin Hood and Jesse James. The Kid embodied youth, romance, nobility, and tragedy. He became someone who was driven by the industrial age into his life of crime. He came to represent the misunderstood, one whose gun was fired at corruption and greed in defense of the poor and downtrodden. He was perceived as making the ultimate sacrifice in the end: martyrdom.

The Wild Bunch. Left to right: Ben Kilpatrick, Harry Longbaugh, Bill Carver, Harvey Logan, and Butch Cassidy.

BUTCH CASSIDY AND THE WILD BUNCH

★ ★ ★

Most outlaws possessed a mean streak, something that, unless checked, zoomed out of control at the slightest provocation. In the days of the cowboy, killing a person was a reflex action, and often the state laws took this into account. After all, to err was human. Billy the Kid had a mean streak, as did Wyatt Earp. In fact, most outlaws could lay claim to having one—except for Butch Cassidy. Butch, though an outlaw, was not mean and, more important, he was not a killer. The only people he killed were a dozen or so Bolivian cavalrymen during his final encounter with the law. Also, Butch was not a petty larcenist; he was a train and bank robber, who apparently was pleasant, friendly, and seemed to genuinely enjoy life. In short, Butch Cassidy was a perfect outlaw hero.

Butch Cassidy was born George Leroy Parker in 1867, the eldest of seven sons, to Mr. and Mrs. Maximillian Parker at their Circle Valley ranch in Utah. The Parker family were devout Mormons. It is said that young George grew up around the ranch and was amiable and hearty of spirit, if unschooled. He was taught the ways of a cowhand by Mike Cassidy, a good-natured cowboy. Cassidy taught young George how to ride and rope cattle, as well as how to shoot and steal cattle and horses. George was a bright student and he soon changed his last name to Cassidy to honor his friend. (He acquired the nickname Butch later.)

Before Mike Cassidy left for Mexico to escape the law, he showed Butch a place that was to serve the boy well most of his life: the

Hole in the Wall, located in northern Wyoming. The Hole in the Wall was accessible only through a narrow, easily defended gorge. The inhabitants of this safe haven were mostly outlaws, but there were a few prostitutes who lived there, too. Butch became familiar with the trail in and out of the Hole in the Wall while riding with Mike Cassidy, who also introduced the fair-haired, good-looking teenager to other desperadoes.

After Mike Cassidy moved to Mexico, Butch moved from his family's ranch to the mining town of Telluride, Colorado, where he not only made a living moving ore down a mountain by mule, but also met and befriended a family by the name of McCarty, who taught him the fine points of robbing banks.

For a while, Butch rode and robbed banks with the McCarty family. He learned to do intelligence work before taking the risk of robbery and to make the company clerk open the vault so that it didn't have to be blown up.

In 1889, Butch planned and took part in the robbery of the San Miguel Valley Bank at Telluride, which netted the group $19,500. Curiously enough, the success of the robbery wasn't enough to spur Butch on to a life of full-time crime—at least not quite yet.

In 1890, when the McCarty gang left their Star Valley (a small area that joins the states of Wyoming and Idaho together) ranch, Butch stayed behind and worked as a cowhand on Wyoming ranches for two years. One of the tricks he perfected during this time was to ride a horse at full gallop past a tree with an ace of spades nailed into it and simultaneously fire four bullets into the center of the ace with his pistol. Butch believed he performed poorly if three out of the four bullets did not go through the center.

In 1892, he worked for a while as a butcher, gaining his nickname, "Butch." This was the last time that he attempted to earn an honest living, and when he was falsely accused of robbing a drunk (charges that were later dropped), he was so humiliated that he set off on his horse and, as the saying goes, never looked back.

Above: The lead actors from the movie Butch Cassidy and the Sundance Kid. *Clockwise, from top, left: Katharine Ross as Etta Place, Robert Redford as Sundance, and Paul Newman as Butch Cassidy. Left: A member of the famous Hole in the Wall Gang, Camelia Hanks.*

they were so successful that the Pinkerton Detective Agency began to concentrate solely on Butch's gang. As William A. Pinkerton wrote to his Denver office: "From reliable information we have received they intend to make railroads and express companies their victims. We must use every facility at our command to break up this criminal organization."

Shortly after this note was transmitted, a stranger by the name of Charles Carter showed up at the Hole in the Wall. Carter appeared shrewd and Butch always was on the lookout for smart gang members. After gaining Butch's confidence, Carter mysteriously disappeared from the hideout. The gang soon discovered that Carter was not an outlaw, but a Pinkerton detective named Siringo. This infiltration cost the gang close to one year's worth of work.

However, there was one person near Star Valley that he would return to speak with from time to time, an elderly lady, one Mrs. Simpson, who lived in the center of the wilderness and was known as the only white woman in that area for several miles. During the winter of 1892, when a severe flu epidemic swept through the community, she needed medicine. Butch took it upon himself to provide it for her and would then sit with her and tell her stories about his experiences in the Badlands. It is said that he was a master at spinning yarns and was able to work a story up to a fever pitch before delivering the ending.

After the brief jail stint in 1892 for robbing horses, Butch was released after giving his word that he would never rob anything in Wyoming for the rest of his life. It is believed that although he masterminded robbing sprees in the state, he did indeed keep his word and did not participate in another robbery there. It was at this time that he returned to his hideout in the Wyoming mountains and assembled a band of outlaws, the Wild Bunch. Butch was a leader and had a flair, it is said, for planning and organizing robberies. It was from this hideout that the gang, under Butch's careful eye, began to primarily rob railway trains, although bank robberies were a close second.

Many of the trains heading eastward carried bank notes or gold, and the Wild Bunch began to enjoy great success at stealing them; in fact,

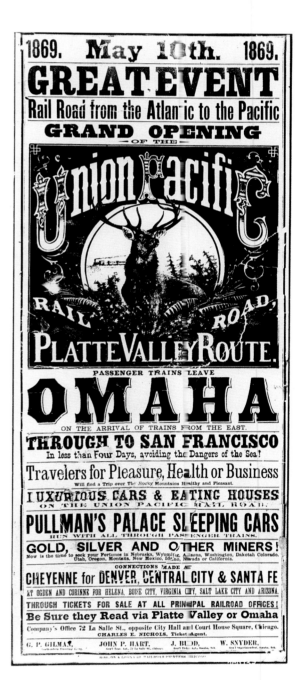

Eventually, Butch realized that the West was becoming rapidly a thing of the past and that his way of life was dying along with it. People were encroaching from all sides, and fences were springing up with the people. The Wild Bunch was soon to be history. Hounded also by the Pinkerton Agency, Butch decided to lay down his gun and met with lawyer Charles Kelly to formulate a pardon for himself. The governor of Utah was approached with a proposal, but he eventually refused it, citing several killings by Butch, which he said could not go unpunished. (As mentioned, most historians agree that, with the exception of the Bolivian soldiers killed in his final shoot-out, Butch had never committed murder. However, during his lengthy career as an outlaw, he had made many enemies, and it is believed that one of these people testified against him). At this time, Cassidy had retreated to the Hole in the Wall.

In 1900, after an unsuccessful attempt at working for the Union Pacific Railroad, Butch returned to robbing banks and then moved to San Antonio, Texas, with his fellow gang member the Sundance Kid; the two lived well in San Antonio for some time until they ran out of money. With most of the gang dead or in jail, Butch and the Sundance Kid decided that the United States was no longer a likely place to earn money. During this time the pair were joined by a girlfriend, Etta Place, and decided to emigrate to South America. After spending several days in New York City, Butch, the Kid, and Etta sailed for Buenos Aires, Argentina, in February 1901.

It is at this point in Cassidy's life that all the facts vanish. Every account one reads of Butch's final years is in conflict with the next. No one actually knows what happened to him. The following is a popular version, one approximated in the film *Butch Cassidy and the Sundance Kid.*

In South America, the three lived well and bought a ranch, which they stocked with thirteen hundred sheep, five hundred head of cattle and thirty-five horses. Soon, however, Butch became restless. Some have expressed the idea that Butch was a compulsive thief, and that the rewards of robbing were secondary to the thrills. Whatever the case may be, Butch and the Kid began to rob banks again.

Sometime during the last year of Butch's life, 1911, it is believed that Etta Place returned to the United States. No one is sure when or why; in fact, no one is even sure that she did.

Butch and Sundance, and a stolen mule bearing the brand of the mining company they had worked for, were sighted in the small town of San Vicente, Bolivia. They had stopped at the town square, perhaps to see if the local bank could be robbed. The Bolivian troops were alerted; they soon encircled the pair and demanded their surrender. Obviously, Butch and Sundance did not relish the idea of spending the rest of their lives in a Bolivian prison. Somehow, a shoot-out ensued and, in the end, both Butch and Sundance lay dead.

Many people mourned the passing of this last great outlaw. He was widely regarded as warm, honest within his own code of ethics, and, above all, a true original.

Paul Newman and Robert Redford pose on the set for Butch Cassidy and the Sundance Kid. *This film version of the Hole in the Wall's exploits was a huge box-office success and resurrected Redford's career. The film was extremely sympathetic to the outlaws.*

CHAPTER

4

ENTERTAINERS

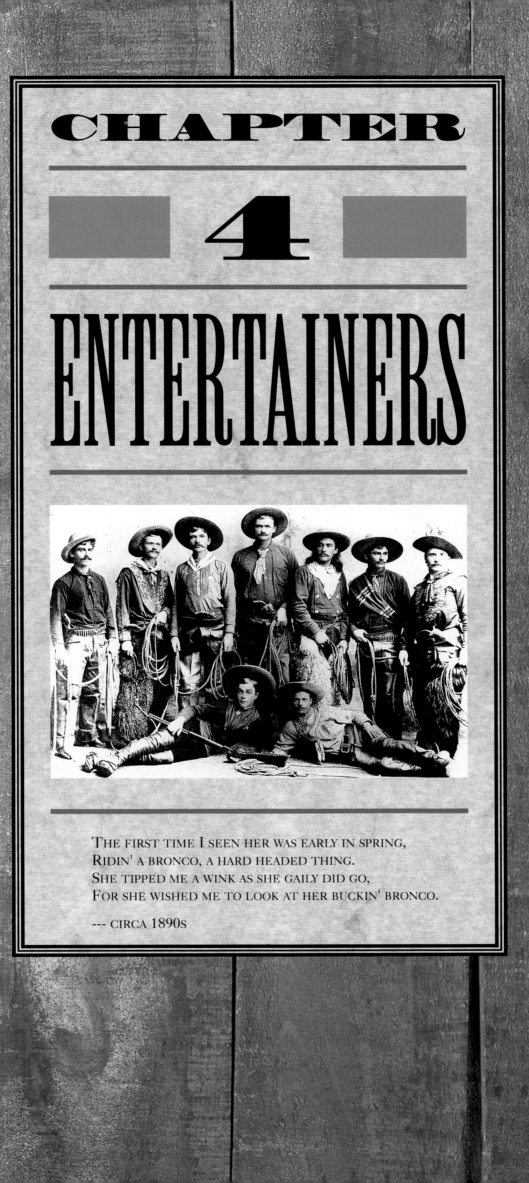

THE FIRST TIME I SEEN HER WAS EARLY IN SPRING,
RIDIN' A BRONCO, A HARD HEADED THING.
SHE TIPPED ME A WINK AS SHE GAILY DID GO,
FOR SHE WISHED ME TO LOOK AT HER BUCKIN' BRONCO.

--- CIRCA 1890s

The whimsical verse on page 71 is from an old cowboy song paraphrased by an unknown songwriter to describe his fascination with a woman riding a bronco in a Wild West show. His experience is like that of thousands of other Americans during the waning years of the Golden West, a time when the open range began to disappear, signaling an end to traditional cowboy life. Nevertheless, before the birth of the Wild West show and the rodeo, citizens of the United States and Europe were not able to view the frontier unless they were part of the movement toward the West. With the advent of the Wild West shows, however, people were able to observe the wildness first-hand from the safety of their seats. While past heroes needed the mountains or the woods to recreate their reality, cowboys and cowgirls were able to recreate theirs with a minimal amount of equipment, specifically an enclosure, a rope, a gun, and a horse.

While many participants in the Wild West shows, such as Buffalo Bill Cody, were indeed experienced in the ways of the frontier, it was also possible to train actors and actresses to play the parts of cowboys, cowgirls, and Indi-

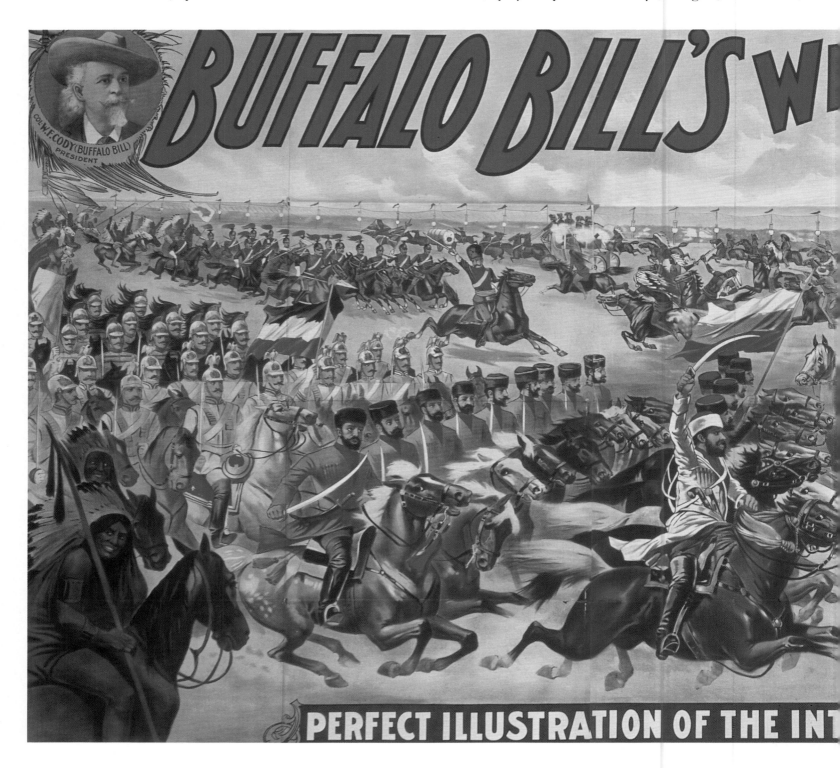

ans. These paid performers were taught by authentic cowboys who were not able otherwise to capitalize on their expertise. Whether the performers were authentic cowboys or not didn't really matter, for audiences generally weren't able to discern the difference between truth and fantasy and if they could, they didn't care. A mass market for cowboy culture developed; quickly the contests and games of working cowboys gave way to trained professional rodeo riders, show actors, and circuslike performers. Audiences clearly craved to see more and more of such spectacles.

No one is certain which came first, the rodeo, which was strictly a series of contests between horse or bull and man, or the Wild West show, which included all of the rodeo, but augmented it with false history and splendid pageantry. Each contains an important component of the other within itself and, in reality, both are tied together. Both began in the 1880s, but women first appeared on the national scene in Buffalo Bill's Wild West show. This show eclipsed all others of its kind and made Bill Cody (Buffalo Bill) the true king of all show cowboys, and Annie Oakley the queen.

This lithograph of Buffalo Bill's Wild West and Congress of Rough Riders of the World illustrates part of the grand pageantry paying customers could expect to see at this famous Wild West show.

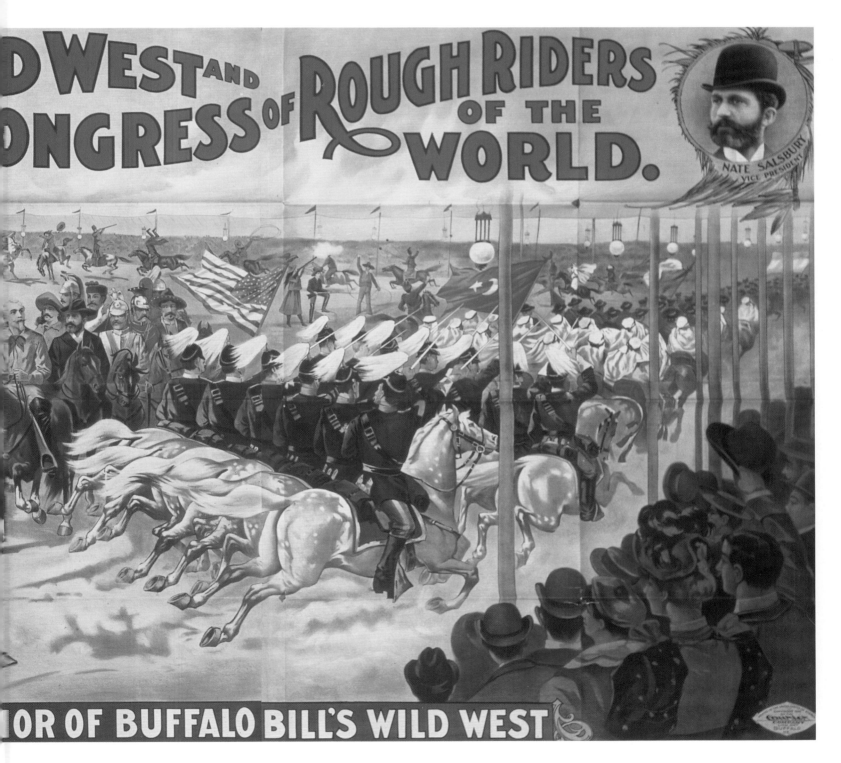

BUFFALO BILL'S WILD WEST SHOW

★ ★ ★

Born William Frederick Cody in North Platte, Nebraska, Bill Cody grew up west of the Missouri. His life history is unknown until the 1860s, when Cody began working on the U.S. Army's supply train during its Utah wars expeditions against the Mormons. He joined in the Colorado gold rush and rode for the Pony Express, as well as scouted for the army during its struggles against the Comanches, Kiowas, Sioux, and nearly every other plains Indian tribe. In the minds of many people of the era, Cody grew up making a living based on the opportunities dictated by his environment. He earned his moniker, Buffalo Bill, by hunting buffalo to feed the construction crews of the Kansas Pacific Railroad.

Right: This photograph capturing some exciting moments from Buffalo Bill's Wild West show is a fine example of what is referred to as "cowboy fun." Americans and Europeans flocked to these shows—and made William Frederick Cody a rich man.

Buffalo Bill's life on the plains before he became a famous American Western hero is almost completely forgotten. What is recalled is that in 1872, he took his first step in his race to fame when he produced and acted in a play, *Scouts of the Plains*, written by his friend Edward Z. C. Judson, alias Ned Buntline, the father of the frontier romance story.

According to Cody's biographer, Richard J. Walsh, Buntline met Cody by accident. Having heard of Major Frank North, the commander of three companies of Pawnee scouts who had been enlisted in the U.S. Army to fight the Sioux, Buntline traveled to Fort McPherson,

Left: A banner displaying several of the participants in Buffalo Bill's Wild West show. Note the picture of Annie Oakley at the center of the banner.

Right: Buffalo Bill with several of his Native-American performers. Below: This 1906 photograph is a good depiction of Buffalo Bill's Wild West. Opposite: Buffalo Bill Cody with his famous horse, White Powder. Buffalo Bill, Daniel Boone, and Kit Carson are considered the fathers of the Wild West, having defended the American Dream against savagery.

Nebraska, in 1869 in order to turn the major into a dime-novel hero. North, however, declined the offer. Instead he exclaimed, "If you want a man to fill that bill, he's over there under the wagon." Of course, the man sleeping under the covered wagon was the almost unknown scout, Buffalo Bill Cody. Buntline spoke with Cody and accompanied him and his large white horse, White Powder, on several scouting expeditions before returning to New York City to create a hero that would sell millions of books to a Western-adventure-hungry audience.

After an unsuccessful attempt to get Buffalo Bill onto the stage to portray his now-famous self, Ned Buntline finally got his wish in December 1872. *Scouts of the Plains* consisted mostly of white men shooting Indians, but it was a hit with audiences. After three years of working with Buntline, Cody, his friend Texas Jack Omohundro, and his press agent/business manager, John M. Burke, organized their own show. It was Burke who began to mold Cody into the legend that lives on today; thus Cody joined the ranks of Daniel Boone and Kit Carson as a man who defended civilization from savagery.

In 1882, Buffalo Bill convinced the ranchers of North Platte, Nebraska, his hometown, to sponsor each year an Independence Day celebration that would be called an "Old Glory Blowout." The events, including rodeo competition and performances of tricks on horseback, later provided the genesis for Cody's Wild West show. Cody's Old Glory Blowout began with a musical overture, played by musicians dressed in flannel shirts, slouch hats, and moccasins, followed by cowboys riding bucking broncos and executing fancy rope tricks. There was a staged Indian attack on the Deadwood Stagecoach during a simulated run, which was, of course, stopped by cowboys. The Pony Express was also exhibited to the thrill of the crowd, and a herd of buffalo was paraded

through as part of the buffalo hunt. This celebration, held the same year that the first rodeo was held in Pecos, Texas, developed into Buffalo Bill's Wild West show in 1883.

ANNIE OAKLEY

Neither rodeos nor Buffalo Bill's Wild West show featured cowgirls as prominent characters, but this changed in 1885, when Annie Oakley, the woman who would be made to later observe in the Rodgers and Hammerstein musical comedy *Annie Get Your Gun*, "You cain't shoot a man in the tail like a quail," joined Buffalo Bill's Wild West show.

Annie Oakley was born Phoebe Ann Moses, but she changed her name to Annie Oakley for no known apparent reason. Annie's birth date is unknown, and no one knows how she and Buffalo Bill met. Certainly, the reputation of a woman who could shoot as well as Annie would easily reach business-minded Buffalo Bill. Annie, before becoming involved in show business with her now famous shooting act, had never set foot west of Cincinnati. This young woman, who knew nothing of cattle, horses, or cowboys, grew to become one of the West's most beloved heroes. Her exploits of feeding her family by trapping and shooting quail and squirrels as well as how she met, had a shooting match with, and later married Frank Butler is affectionately if speculatively chronicled in *Annie Get Your Gun*.

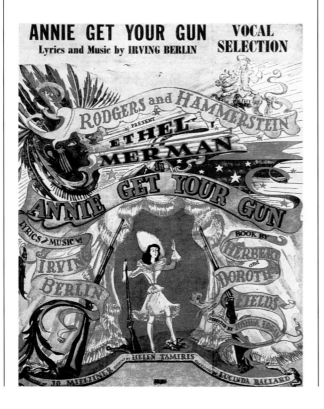

Annie's exploits with guns were not the only things that endeared her to audiences worldwide. At first, she did very little else but perform with her rifle and six-shooter. Soon, however, she began to combine her skills as a shootist with her sense of drama and charming personality. Her biographer, Dexter Fellows, commented on Annie's allure:

Even before her name was on the lips of every man, woman, and child in America, the sight of this frail girl among the rough plainsmen seldom failed to inspire enthusiastic plaudits. Her entrance was always a very pretty one. She never walked. She tripped in, bowing, waving, and wafting kisses. Her first few shots brought forth a few screams of fright from the women, but they were soon lost in round after round of applause. It was she who set the audience at ease and prepared it for the continuous crack of firearms which followed.

Opposite: Buffalo Bill's Wild West was a big hit in England, where the company often played to royalty. Here Buffalo Bill poses with some of the cast from the show in front of the Deadwood stagecoach in London. Above: "Little Sure Shot" Annie Oakley poses with her rifle. The nickname was given to her by Chief Sitting Bull, who quite liked the diminutive rodeo star. Left: The frontispiece to the sheet music from the highly successful Broadway musical Annie Get Your Gun.

SITTING BULL.

Annie's shooting tricks consisted of hitting glass balls and clay pigeons with rifle bullets. One particular crowd-pleaser was a trick that consisted of Annie throwing small three-by-five-inch (7.5-by-12.5-cm) cards high into the air, then slicing them in half with bullets. Each card had a picture of her on it and a big red heart. After she split the cards, she tossed them into the crowd, to the delight of all.

It was Chief Sitting Bull who affectionately christened Annie "Little Sure Shot," although Annie combined a sense of femininity with her strength. For example, between performances, she was often seen creating fine needlepoint embroidery. It is also said that when introduced to the Prince of Wales, Annie rebuffed protocol and the prince and, instead, greeted the princess with a warm handshake. This individualistic behavior is said to have provoked the prince to utter that he wished there "were more women in the world like her."

CHIEF SITTING BULL

Chief Sitting Bull joined the Wild West show in 1885, although he only toured with the show for that season. Because he had seen Annie Oakley during the previous year and had taken a genuine liking to her, he had agreed to tour with the show; however, it was difficult for the heroic Sioux chief to fit into the show's context of savage Indians and righteous white settlers, particularly since the show depicted the final charge against Custer—Sitting Bull was, of course, Custer's enemy and consequently, seen as the source of the cavalry's troubles. When Sitting Bull would come out dressed in his full beautiful ceremonial feathers, he was booed by audiences. During the year that he toured with the Wild West show, it is said that he never understood why wealthy white men allowed such poverty in their society. Therefore, Sitting Bull instantly turned over his weekly salary of fifty dollars to the multitude of bootblacks and poor children who gravitated to the show.

★ ★ ★

During its peak years (1883–1905), Buffalo Bill's Wild West show was made more international. Famous Hispanic cowboys, including two noteworthy Texans, Antonio "Champion Vaquero Rider" Esquival and José "Mexican Joe" Berrara, who performed intricate rope tricks, joined the show, which also featured riders dressed as Argentinian gauchos.

In 1887, Buffalo Bill packed up his two hundred actors and three hundred head of livestock and sailed to England, where the troupe performed for Queen Victoria's Golden Jubilee. After returning to the United States in 1889, the company began a four-year tour of North America. During this time, there were at least a dozen women performing regularly in Buffalo Bill's Wild West show. Some were part of a skit that featured an Indian raid on a settler's log cabin, while others performed tricks on horseback.

Because Buffalo Bill's show enjoyed tremendous success, it was soon copied by other troupes. One such imitator was Pawnee Bill's Historical Wild West Show (organized by Gordon W. Lillie, known as Pawnee Bill), which featured a woman, May Lillie, in its shooting act. Ms. Lillie, who grew up in a Pennsylvania

Opposite: Chief Sitting Bull poses in native dress with a beaded pouch and a war club. During Sitting Bull's tenure at Buffalo Bill's Wild West, he would often give away his weekly salary to the poor who flocked to the show. Below: Buffalo Bill's Wild West did much to create cowboy fashion. From left to right, three actors from the show: Joe Esquival, Dick Johnson, and Jim Kid.

Right: Gordon W. Lillie (Pawnee Bill) displays the look that would make him a celebrity in a spin-off Wild West show. By the late 1890s some 116 such shows toured the United States. Below: May Lillie on her horse. In 1887 Lillie was a gold-medal winner in a rifle-shooting contest held in Philadelphia. She was one of the early female stars of the Wild West shows. Opposite: This program (circa 1890) from Pawnee Bill's Wild West show attempts to lure customers in much the same way as advertisements do today—by using pretty women and action, and suggesting the exotic.

Quaker community and was a graduate of Smith College, married Pawnee Bill. In 1887, she was the gold-medal winner in a rifle-shooting contest in Philadelphia, and again in 1889 in Atlanta, Georgia. By 1893, Pawnee's group numbered some three hundred men and women. The women were billed as "beauteous, dashing, daring and laughing Western girls who ride better than any other women in the world."

During the late 1890s through the early 1900s, it is believed that imitators of Buffalo Bill's show numbered some 116, and most, if not all, included women in their programs, following the example of Buffalo Bill Cody.

Other Notable Performers

★ ★ ★

CALAMITY JANE

Right: Three veterans of the Wild West enjoying a conversation about old times. From left to right: C.S. Stobie (known as "Mountain Charlie"), Calamity Jane, and Jack Crawford. Below: Calamity Jane poses in the leather pants that she helped to make acceptable as women's attire.

Another woman made famous by the Western show was Calamity Jane. Calamity Jane, born either Mary Jane Canary or Martha Jane Cannary, was reputed to have had a prostitute for a mother and was said to have been an alcoholic herself. By the age of seventeen, the rebellious Jane discarded her dresses and began wearing trousers and associating with railroad construction work crews. A few years later, while with General Crook on his expedition against the

Sioux nation, Calamity was sent packing after being discovered swimming nude with the men of the expedition.

During the 1880s, Calamity Jane travelled from Wild West show to Wild West show, wearing fashionable Western gear and performing various stunts with six-shooters and rifles. Jane was one of the first women to become famous for wearing leather pants and, not surprisingly, being extremely boisterous. She often wore beaded leggings and smoked cigars.

During her own lifetime, Jane became immortalized in the dime novels of the era. The novels, however, depicted Jane as a woman of breeding who could drop her dialect at will and speak perfect English, while they magnified her ability to ride and fire her six-shooter at the same time. Such was the price of fame. In the end, she disappeared the way she came— mysteriously.

BILL PICKETT

Many say that the greatest cowboy showman of all time was Bill Pickett, a black cowboy from Texas. Pickett first attained fame as a cowhand on Oklahoma's famous Miller and Lux 101 Ranch, which, during the 1890s, was one of

Calamity Jane

the United States' eminent cattle ranches. During this time, the 101 Ranch was also the center of one of the most successful Wild West and rodeo shows, and Bill Pickett was one of its major stars.

Bill Pickett was a bulldogger. In other words, he wrestled bulls to the ground. In Fred Gipson's book on the 101 ranch, *The Fabulous Empire*, he describes Bill Pickett like this:

The way Bill went at it, he piled out of his saddle onto the head of a running steer, sometimes jumping five or six feet [1.5 to 2 m] to tie on. He'd grab a horn in each hand and twist them till the steer's nose came up. Then he'd reach in and grab the steer's upper lip with his strong white teeth, throw up his hands to show he wasn't holding anymore, and fall to one side of the steer, dragging along beside him until the animal went down.

Another account of Pickett's notoriety is a turn-of-the-century 101 Ranch rodeo performance in New York's Madison Square Garden. Since New York audiences were not accustomed to seeing rodeos, the first evening's performance was poorly attended. That night,

when the steer that Pickett was to bulldog cleared its chute, it reacted adversely to the situation, charged a six-foot (2-m) fence, and blindly went into the grandstand. Pickett, on his horse, also jumped the fence, and followed the bull into the small crowd. At the time, Will Rogers was hazing (distracting the bull from the cowhand, if necessary) for Pickett, and Rogers, apparently not wishing to be outdone himself, also took his horse over the board fence into the seats. While the customers were screaming, Pickett rode down the bull, leaped from his horse, sunk his teeth into the steer's lip, and dragged him down. At that moment, Will Rogers threw a lasso over the steer's hind legs and, with Pickett still attached by his teeth to the steer, dragged the yowling animal and the cowboy back into the arena. The press picked up the story, and the Garden was filled to capacity for the remainder of the shows.

Above: Bill Pickett posing with a lasso. Many say that Pickett was the best cowboy showman ever. During his lifetime he entertained audiences on both sides of the Atlantic with his bulldogging antics. Left: Will Rogers and his famous smile. Early on, Rogers often hazed (distracted the bull from the cowhand) for cowboys engaged in bulldogging.

While an unidentified Native-American woman watches, Bill Pickett, participating in the 101 Ranch rodeo, shows off his skills.

Another story of Pickett's exploits occurred in 1908, when the Millers, who were running the 101 Ranch at the time, decided to take their show to Mexico City. They arrived during a fiesta; unaware of the importance of bullfighting to the Mexicans, Miller's group created an aura of hostility by telling local newspapers that Bill Pickett's bulldogging act was "a greater show than any bullfight." Joseph Miller announced that Pickett could single-handedly throw two steers in the time that it would take for two Mexican bullfighters to throw one. When no one accepted the offer, counteroffers were made and, eventually, a contest was set up. The two groups that had assembled bet on whether Bill Pickett could hold on to one of the fighting bulls for five minutes. This event was to be added to the regularly scheduled show a few days later, and the winning side was to be given five thousand pesos.

On the scheduled day of the contest, the stands at the arena were full of angry Mexicans who booed and hissed when Pickett appeared on his horse. When the bull was released from its chute, Pickett attempted to work his horse in close to the bull, but the steed absolutely refused. Tiring of the animal's resistance, Pickett quickly slid backward off the horse and grabbed the steer's horns. "For the next several minutes," according to an eyewitness account by Fred Gipson, "the bull made a whipcracker out of Bill Pickett. He slammed the Negro's [sic] body against the arena wall. He threw up his head to sling the man right and left, trying to dislodge him. He whipped him against another wall. He reached with his forefeet and tried to pry him loose. Finally, he got down on his knees and drove his sharp horns into the ground, time and again, trying to run Bill through."

The bull was, however, being worn down by the determined Pickett, who held his own until the angry crowd began to hurl beer bottles at him. When a bottle hit him in his ribs, Pickett loosened his grip; afterward, all he could do was hold on for his life as the enraged bull began to toss him around the ring. After six minutes had elapsed, one minute past the agreed time, it became obvious that the Mexican officials were not going to blow the whistle to signal the end of the contest. The men of the 101 rode into the arena and roped the bull while the crowd threw everything within their reach at Pickett until Mexican soldiers intervened, and Joseph Miller's group collected their money.

Bill Pickett survived for many years after this incident, which added incredible fame to his already large reputation. The Miller 101 show continued with Pickett as its star until August 1914, when during a London engagement, World War I began in England. Under a national emergency order, the British Crown seized all the troupe's stock except six horses and one wagon.

The 101 Ranch, like most other southwestern ranches, was depleted during World War I, and further so by the combined drought and depression of the 1930s. In 1932, Pickett, then in his seventies, was the only surviving ranch hand still employed on the once-thriving 101. He had gone out to the corral to cut some horses out of the small herd in the pen. This was routinely done in order to reshoe or check on a certain horse. A large sorrel reared up, its hoof grazed Pickett's head and knocked him to the ground. The sorrel then stomped Pickett and fractured his skull. Eleven days later, this great cowboy died. He was buried on a high knoll overlooking the ranch he loved so much.

Many have said that Pickett's lip-biting technique earned him the right to say that he invented bulldogging. Whether or not he invented it, Bill Pickett won over audiences in America and Europe. Ever since, the sport of bulldogging has appeared as a rodeo sport, even though today's practitioners have given up the lip-biting technique and have instead adopted leverage to drop the steer.

Bill Pickett displaying the bulldogging technique that would earn him a place in the Cowboy Hall of Fame.

THE TELEVISION WESTERN
★ ★ ★

The Lone Ranger riding his horse Silver. The Lone Ranger was one of many cowboy shows that created mythic heroes (in this case a Texas Ranger) that people the world over would attempt to emulate.

Although its beginning during the 1955–1956 season was quiet and almost unheralded, *Gunsmoke* soon proved to be a highly popular program and influenced the style of the television Western, a form of entertainment that was still in its infancy. Prior to this program, television Westerns were for children and included such shows as *The Lone Ranger* and *Hopalong Cassidy*. These children's Westerns created a mythological heroic status for the protagonist.

Gunsmoke, starring James Arness as Marshal Matt Dillon, addressed adult issues and relationships. Marshal Dillon did

not seem to enjoy the necessary violence of his job, but accepted it as a necessity while he focused on the interpersonal aspects of his dangerous work. Part of the reason for this adult orientation is that Hollywood film studios became involved in planning the shows, which allowed for greater depth of character due to improved scripts and more talented actors. Within a year, shows such as *Wagon Train*, *The Virginian*, and *Bonanza* began to thrive and continue for many seasons.

Because of the success of *Gunsmoke*, and the other adult Westerns, a newer wave of Western soon took the place of the scandal-ridden quiz shows, many of which were pulled off the air during the 1958–1959 season. Soon, Westerns created an anti-hero who, while guided by self-interest, devoted his time and strength to helping others who were less strong and more in

The Hopalong Cassidy radio was a popular item for listening to the weekly exploits of America's cowboy heroes. Today it is considered quite collectible.

need. Such hit shows as *Maverick*, *Sugarfoot*, and *Have Gun Will Travel* are prime examples of this genre.

These shows remained popular until the 1960s, when "oaters," as Westerns are called in the industry, were too abundant and competition was too great, thereby leaving no room for new shows. America was also beginning to examine violence on television. The U.S. Congress began to study Westerns (as well as other outlaw shows, such as *The Untouchables*) and the networks began to pull away from the Western due to the pressure to reduce violence. Finally, demographic studies of television audiences began to reveal that adult Westerns were favored by an older audience, while children and young adults preferred situation comedies. Because young adults and children were the larger

audience, advertisers began to support sitcoms. Sadly, *Gunsmoke* was pulled off the air in the mid-1970s, a casualty of modern marketing.

Top: Actor Richard Boone poses with his hand on his six-shooter. The star of the hugely popular television series Have Gun Will Travel, *Boone's character, Paladin, dispensed justice while quoting Shelley, Byron, or Shakespeare. Left: The men from* Bonanza. *Even today these shows are popular in syndication. Clearly, they have tapped into America's vision of itself.*

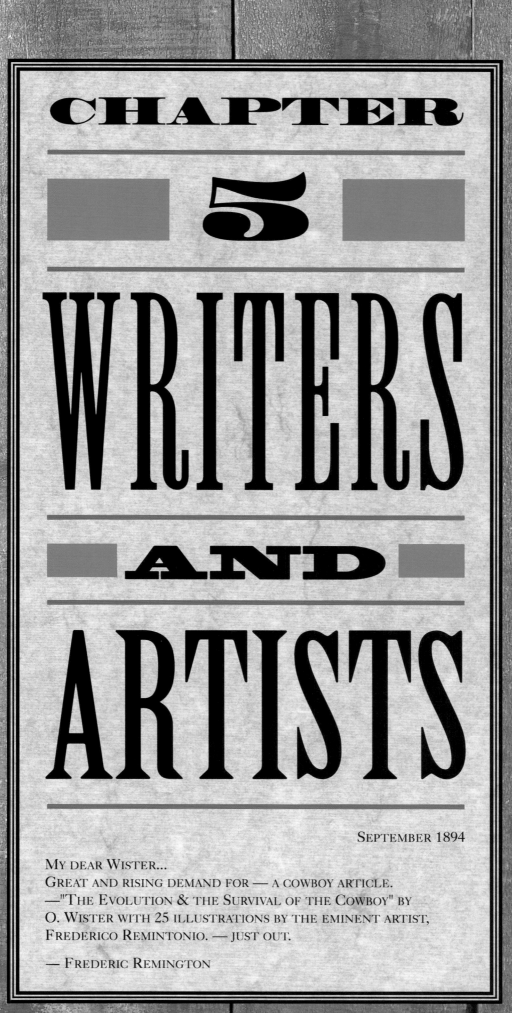

CHAPTER 5 WRITERS AND ARTISTS

SEPTEMBER 1894

MY DEAR WISTER...
GREAT AND RISING DEMAND FOR — A COWBOY ARTICLE.
—"THE EVOLUTION & THE SURVIVAL OF THE COWBOY" BY
O. WISTER WITH 25 ILLUSTRATIONS BY THE EMINENT ARTIST,
FREDERICO REMINTONIO. — JUST OUT.

— FREDERIC REMINGTON

Above: Owen Wister. He, among others, helped to fashion a national hero who would embody the best and the worst the United States had to offer. Right: Another famous cowboy author, Andy Adams.

cigarette advertisements to popular fashion, songs, and jargon, cowboys and the Wild West are deeply embedded in our culture.

How did a wage-earning cowpuncher, someone whose activities actually contributed very little to the scheme of things during the time of the Golden West, provide the stuff from which legends are made? Certainly, the cowboy is a symbol for many things—individualism, courage, chivalry, and honor, to name a few—that have little foundation in fact; however, what the cowboy was is less important than what he was thought to have been, for he symbolizes America's image of itself. And while historians will slowly displace the errors about the lives of the frontier men and women, popular culture continues to romantically speculate on what our past could have been.

Without a doubt, cowboys, with the exception of Buffalo Bill Cody and a handful of others, did not have the desire or the means to make heroes of themselves. While many authors, such as Charles Siringo, a former cowboy, tried to exploit the cowboy, their works did not reach the heroic proportions that *The Log of a Cowboy* or *The Virginian* did. However, chroniclers of cowboy culture, whether they were entertainers or artists, shared a common viewpoint: they presented the cowboy in a

The letter on page 91 to Owen Wister, a cowboy author, from Frederic Remington, a cowboy illustrator, was written in 1894, but it could have been penned in the 1990s, for the cowboy is still the predominant character in United States mythology. The cowboy, much more than the trapper, soldier, explorer, or even homesteader, typified the American Western experience in the popular mind of the nineteenth and twentieth centuries.

There are many authors, such as Andy Adams, writer of the classic *The Log of a Cowboy* (1903), or Owen Wister, writer of *The Virginian* (1903), who are responsible for the cowboy receiving increasingly greater critical attention, while illustrators such as Frederic Remington and Charles Russell created drawings that idealized the cowboy, portraying him as strong and virile; these illustrations are still popular—and quite valuable. The cowboy image is ever-present: from film to military code, from

An illustration from Owen Wister's book, The Virginian. *This novel was an early example of popular culture romanticizing the past. Novels such as this displaced the truth and created a new past where settlers could envision themselves as heroes fighting a noble battle.*

context that was completely separate from historical reality. If they did not invent the cowboy, then they did indeed invent his persona, his desires, his love life, and the sun-sinks-in-the-West happy ending.

Buffalo Bill Cody was the first to transform the cowboy into a salable commodity. The success of his Wild West show is a testament to that achievement. Buffalo Bill also took a six-foot-five (192.5-cm) Texas cowpuncher by the name of William Levi Taylor and, in 1884, introduced him to audiences as Buck Taylor, the "King of Cowboys."

Cody's action was important for several reasons. At the time of Cody's promoting Taylor as the "King of Cowboys," cowboys themselves were the victim of what we refer to today

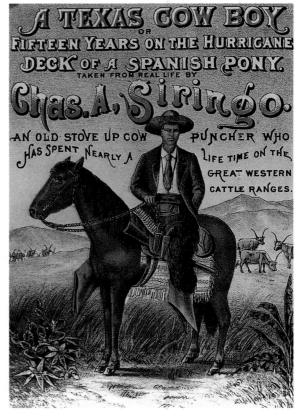

Right: This illustration was used as the second frontispiece for the first edition and the sole frontispiece for the second edition of Charles A. Siringo's A Texas Cowboy. *Below: Charles A. Siringo, the extremely popular cowboy author, often wrote realistic portrayals of the difficult life of a cowboy on the range.*

as bad press. Writers of the day did not view cowboys favorably in the least. In fact, they saw cowboys as drunken rowdies who were one step away from being vagabond degenerates and who had no respect for private property—thereby making life utterly miserable for unsuspecting and peace-loving city folk who were terrified by these rambunctious goings-on. Cody carefully managed Buck Taylor's career and shaped his image, that of a young Texan who seemed to long for the idyllic life on the Great Plains. By promoting Taylor as a gentle giant who loved children, Cody did a great deal to transform the public's perception of cowboys.

As Taylor's career flourished with his image, so too did the country's interest in cowboys. In 1887 Prentiss Ingraham published *Buck Taylor, King of the Cowboys,* and Erastus Beadle's Dime Novel Library published *The Raiders and the Rangers: A Story of the Wild and Thrilling Life of William L. Taylor,* making Taylor the first cowboy hero in fiction. Spin-offs of other characters from these books were soon produced, creating stories of men with names like Buckskin Sam. From here on, the cowboy was portrayed as a hero on the page and on canvas. Here then is a selection of those writers and artists whose work was critical to shaping the cowboy legend.

A Cowboy at Work

★ ★ ★

"After a month's hard work we had the eleven hundred head of wild and woolly steers ready to turn over to the Muckleroy outfit at Thirteen Mile Point on the Mustang, where they were camped, ready to receive them. Their outfit consisted mostly of Kansas 'short horns,' which they had brought back with them the year before.

"It was a cold, rainy evening when the cattle were counted and turned over to Tom Merril. Henry Coats, Geo. Gifford and myself were the only boys who were almost worn out standing night guard half of every night for the past month and then starting in with a fresh outfit made it appear tough to us.

"That night it began to storm terribly. The herd began to drift early and by midnight we were five or six miles [8 or 10 km] from camp. The steers showed a disposition to stampede but we handled them easy and sang melodious songs which kept them quieted. But about one o'clock they stampeded in grand shape. One of the 'short horns,' a long-legged fellow by the name of Saint Clair got lost from the herd and finally when he heard the singing came dashing through the herd at full speed yelling 'let 'em slide, we'll stay with 'em!' at every jump.

"They did slide enough, but he failed to 'stay with 'em.' For towards morning one of the boys came across him lying in the grass sound asleep. When he came dashing through the herd a stampede followed; the herd split up into a dozen different bunches—each bunch going in a different direction. I found myself all alone with about three hundred of the frightened steers. Of course all I could do was to keep in front or in the lead and try to check them up. I finally about three o'clock got them stopped and after singing a few 'lullaby' songs they all lay down and went to snoring.

"After the last steer dropped down I concluded I would take a little nap too, so locking both legs around the saddle-horn and lying over on the tired pony's rump, with my left arm for a pillow, while the other still held the bridle-reins, I fell asleep."

—Charles A. Siringo,
Riata and Sours: The Story of a Lifetime Spent in the Saddle

Although life on the range is often romanticized, the work of a cowboy was difficult and required great stamina.

JAMES FENIMORE COOPER

★ ★ ★

At the beginning of the nineteenth century, James Fenimore Cooper created one of the greatest Western figures of all time—a frontier trapper and scout who moves from youth to death through a succession of novels, and who has a different name as he matures: Leatherstocking, Deerslayer, Pathfinder, Natty Bumppo, and Hawkeye. In the series of novels, this trapper/scout was not called a hero, since only men born of the upper classes could be so called in the nineteenth century. Cooper's stories revolve around young white officers of good birth and innocent, young, pale women who faint when the going gets tough.

Cooper based parts of his novel *The Last of the Mohicans* on a well-documented escapade of Daniel Boone, who rescued Betsy Callaway and Jemima Boone, his daughter, from the Cherokees. As the character Cora Munro does in Cooper's novel, so too in reality did Betsy Callaway attempt to help her rescuers by breaking twigs and leaving them behind to mark the trail. The final rescue by Boone also appears in Cooper's novel.

Cooper's novel *The Prairie* chronicles the migration of Americans from Ohio and Kentucky across the Mississippi River following the Louisiana Purchase in 1803. Here, too, Boone appears among the 1804 emigrants. Cooper's description of the migration calls to mind the parting of the Red Sea by Moses:

This adventurous and venerable patriarch was now seen making his last remove; placing the "endless river" between him and the multitude, his own success had drawn around him, and seeking for the renewal of enjoyments which were rendered worthless in his eyes, when trammelled by the forms of human institutions.

Even as early as 1825 a keen but unknown writer for the *Niles' Register* recognized the close resemblance between Boone and Leatherstocking, even after Cooper's hero had appeared in only one story, *The Pioneers*. This writer pointed out that both Boone and Leatherstocking were passionate about the freedom of the forest, loved hunting, and abhorred the ordinary pursuits of civilized society. He went on to point out that Leatherstocking, like Boone, was a symbol of anarchic freedom from restraint and law.

In Cooper's early work, much was made about Leatherstocking's low social status. Later, in *The Last of the Mohicans* and *The Prairie*, which deal mostly with Indian warfare and the rescue of damsels in distress, the old hunter's status in society is not important. In these texts, the hunter's expertise with tracking and his rifle are foremost in the story. Readers today have little interest in the genteel characters of Alice and Duncan, who are technically the heroes, and who held the greatest interest for readers at the time the book was written. The center of the modern reader's attention is Hawkeye, the tracker-scout, who stands between the Indian and the white settler, a synthesis of the best of both cultures. Later, in *The Prairie*, Hawkeye is dying; seated and facing west in his last moments, he says, "I am without kith or kin in the wide world. . . . We have never been chiefs; but honest, and useful in our way. I hope it cannot be denied we have always proved ourselves."

Cooper did not attempt to revolutionize the traditional novel, but instead occupied himself with modifying it as much as possible without actually destroying it. At the same time, he greatly altered his subject matter in order to fit the form he used to tell his frontier stories that have survived the test of time. Toward the end of his twenty-five-year writing career, Cooper wrote a novel with a true Western hero in *The Oak Openings*. This story, although considered to be one of his weakest, finally creates a hero who is not an upper-class gentleman, but a man of the wilderness. Because of writers like James Fenimore Cooper, it became possible for Western men of common birth to be viewed as true romantic heroes.

ERASTUS BEADLE

★ ★ ★

Twenty years later, the hunter-scout of James Fenimore Cooper was slightly modified to appeal to a larger arena of American popular culture through the pages of the dime novel. The dime novel often combined a florid writing style and a new literary device. The frontiersman would in reality be an upper-class man, who was attempting to hide his social stature. The dime-novel writers created characters who were stereotypical and, therefore, well known to audiences. These novels served the same purpose to their usually young audiences as do soap operas today. Both create a comfortable reality where we are permitted to safely love and hate.

In 1858, Erastus Beadle and his brother Irwin, natives of New York State (as was Cooper), and successful publishers in Buffalo, moved to New York City to launch an even more successful publishing venture with the help of a business partner, Robert Adams, of cheap orange-backed paperback books for the mass audience. Although the publishing house of Beadle and Adams was not the first to market inexpensive paperbound novels, they were the first to issue them in series form and in large quantities. Whether they knew it or not, Beadle and Adams had tapped into something very big by making entertainment cheap and easily available.

These novels, which usually consisted of about thirty thousand words, were tailored after the thrillers published in Boston, Massachusetts, by Gleason and Ballou during the 1840s. The thrillers were tales of life in the East during the mid-nineteenth century. Typically, a woman was endangered by a villain, and a handsome, educated, and upper-class Anglo man would come to her rescue. In the end, the couple would be married or get engaged. Beadle's stories had a greater emphasis on their Western setting. Erastus Beadle was a persistent man who developed a systematic devotion to the principles of big business and the belief, even then, that Boston would yield to New York City as the publishing mecca of the United States. Beadle's editor was Orville Vic-

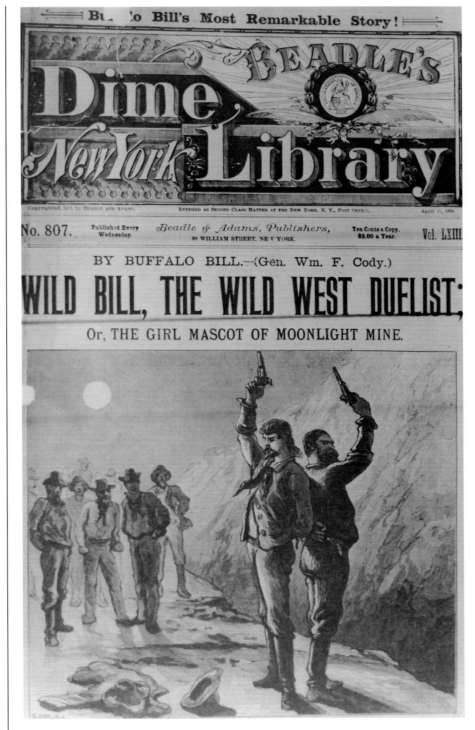

tor, a former newspaperman from Sandusky, Ohio. Victor would supervise the production of dime novels and other series stories for three more decades.

In 1860, Beadle printed the first of his dime novels, *Malaeska: The Indian Wife of the White Hunter*, written by a Mrs. Ann S. Stephens. The eighth story of the series, Edward S. Ellis's *Seth Jones, or the Captives of the Frontier* confirmed that Beadle had tapped a large vein in popular culture, for the book sold as many as

The cover to a dime novel published by Erastus Beadle. The first of these novels was published in 1860.

four hundred thousand copies. Beadle continued printing novel after novel, one series after another, although each story was complete unto itself. In 1865 the normal print run for a dime novel was sixty thousand, but many titles were reprinted over and over again. Between 1860 and 1865, Beadle's total sales approached 5 million copies, and several authors turned out as many as six hundred novels. In nineteenth-century America, success like this was simply awesome. Clearly, an audience that had not been known to exist was discovered for fiction.

As discoverers and promoters of a genre, Beadle and Victor rank among the best. They realized that large-scale production demanded a regular, easily recognizable product; they achieved this by employing standard packaging: the orange-backed paperback as well as various book series that had characteristic for-

mats. Along with a standard story formula, perfected by Victor, any number of writers could churn out copy for the publisher, and when the market altered slightly, the product did, too. Many have said that Orville Victor had an intuitive sense of the direction and nature of popular taste. It is said that authors such as Prentiss Ingraham produced more than six hundred novels, as well as plays and short stories. Ingraham is reported to have turned out a thirty-five-thousand-word tale in a single twenty-four-hour period. While it can be argued that writing like this creates fiction devoid of any literary merit, it is also true that such effort creates work that becomes a mass reverie, like modern soap operas or comic books, the present-day equivalent of the dime novel that Beadle perfected.

Seth Jones, the publishing house's first great success, was set in the late-eighteenth-century frontier village of New York, a locale similar to that of Cooper's stories. In *Seth Jones,* a white girl is captured by Mohawk Indians and is eventually rescued by the rugged and handsome hunter-scout, Seth Jones. A lovable eastern Yankee, Seth knew the wilderness and its inhabitants almost intimately. Said to have been "the perfect Dime Novel" by Orville Victor, Ellis's *Seth Jones* fools the reader until the end of the story, when the reader discovers that the seasoned hunter who has captured the center of attention is no other than the well-bred young Eugene Morton in clever disguise. While the pretext for this disguise is almost laughable (Eugene was off fighting the Indians and believed that his sweetheart no longer loved him), the reader easily recognizes the handy device of combining the appeal of a Wild West figure with the upper-class genteel gentleman to create a popular hero. (Ellis, by the way, continued to be a prolific writer for Beadle's dime novels, and his ease with handling stereotypical characters who were loved by readers continued to sell books. A story of his, *Kent, the Ranger,* first published in 1860, was reprinted for the third time as late as 1877.)

Although the West was not the only setting for the dime novel, it was certainly the most popular. Of the 3,158 dime novels published by Beadle between 1860 and 1898, some two-thirds of the sales occurred west of the Missis-

Below: One of Beadle's half-dime novels. This New York–based publisher helped to define a fiction genre that remains a multi-million-dollar industry today. Opposite: William "Buffalo Bill" Cody posing for the camera before one of his Wild West shows.

William "Big Foot" Wallace sits with his rifle and a smile. As cowboys eclipsed other heroes in the late 1860s, the myth-making machine turned out more and more hard-life stories. The reading public voraciously devoured them all, including Wallace's.

sippi. While the hunter-scout-tracker was at first the favorite character of the dime novel's readers, he was eventually replaced by the outlaw and soldier. However, after 1880, the cowboy eclipsed all these heroes. Seth Jones and Daniel Boone were displaced by characters such as Buffalo Bill Cody, Deadwood Dick, Big Foot Wallace, Wild Bill Hickok, and Calamity Jane. These Beadle characters did not have Cooper's genteel restraints; these Westerners were clearly the heroes of their stories. While dime novelists under Beadle used real people as models, they did not worry about truth or detail; Beadle had instructed his writers that he did not desire "repetition of any experience which, though true, is yet better untold."

The stories, therefore, reflected what the publisher believed was audience need, and they transmitted to hundreds of thousands of people what many thought was true and significant about the West. In other words, the dime novel created a mass cowboy culture.

PULP WESTERNS THRIVE

★ ★ ★

In 1902, Owen Wister published *The Virginian*, a novel that earned, albeit grudgingly, praise from literary critics. In his novel, Wister brought together eastern civility and western roughness and implied virility, a combination that appealed to the American audience of the new century. According to Henry N. Smith, a critic, *The Virginian*, with its larger-than-life hero, its western landscapes, violence, and love story, represented "that last pioneer nobleman, roaming a frontier beyond the dominion of a mother culture in the East, representing both its rebellious runaway sons and its most poignant dream of manhood and freedom."

In 1903, Andy Adams published *The Log of a Cowboy*. Critics and audiences alike realized that Adams had truly created a story that was different, in fact, far more realistic. For Adams was a writer who perhaps knew the cowboy better than anyone else who had previously attempted to write about his culture; first, his stories were partly autobiographical and sec-ond, he incorporated others' experiences as much as possible. In *The Log of a Cowboy*, Adams, like other writers of his ilk, exercised considerable literary license; however, Adams was extremely concerned with the true details of trail driving. His writing reflected this and appealed to those who sought realism in their cowboy fiction. In his later books, Adams explored other aspects of cowboy life, such as the cowboy penchant for storytelling in *Cattle Brands: A Collection of Western Camp-Fire Stories*. The following excerpt is taken from "Around the Spade Wagon," a tale that is in this collection.

They were singing over at one of the wagons across the draw, and after the song ended, Bradshaw asked, "What ever became of Raneka Bill Hunter?"

"Oh, he's drifting about," said Edwards. "Mouse here can tell you about him. They're old college chums."

This drawing by Frederic Remington depicts one of the daily pastimes of the small, and often slow, frontier towns, a game of Monte. This drawing was printed in Owen Wister's The Virginian.

"*Raneka was working for the '-B Q' people last summer," said Mouse, "but was discharged for hanging a horse, or rather he discharged himself. It seems that someone took a fancy to a horse in his mount. The last man to buy into an outfit that way always gets all the bad horses for his string. As Raneka was a new man there, the result was that some excuse was given him to change, and they rung in a spoilt horse on him in changing. Being new that way, he wasn't on to the horses. The first time he tried to saddle this new horse he showed up bad. The horse trotted up to him when the rope fell on his neck, reared up nicely and playfully, and threw out his forefeet, stripping the three upper buttons off Bill's vest pattern. Bill never said a word about his intentions, but tied him to the corral fence and saddled up his own private horse. There were several men around camp, but they said nothing, being party to a deal, though they noticed Bill riding away with the spoilt horse. He took him down on the creek about a mile from camp and hung him.*

"*How did he do it? Why, there was a big cottonwood grew on a bluff bank of the creek. One limb hung out over the bluff, over the bed of the creek. He left the running noose on the horse's neck, climbed out on this overhanging limb, taking the rope through a fork directly over the water. He then climbed down and snubbed the free end of the rope to a small tree, and began taking in his slack. When the rope began to choke the horse, he reared and plunged, throwing himself over the bluff. That settled his ever hurting any one. He was hung higher than Haman. Bill never went back to the camp, but struck out for other quarters. There was a month's*

wages coming to him, but he would get that later or they might keep it. Life had charms for an old-timer like Bill, and he didn't hanker for any reputation as a bronco-buster. It generally takes a verdant to pine for such honors."

The Log of a Cowboy was a novel; however, it had no plot but merely consisted of episodic ramblings of cowboys discussing life on the range. It was a true picture of cowboy life, and centered on a cattle drive from the Rio Grande to northwestern Montana in 1882. Although many criticized the book for being dull, the truth, at least according to Adams's account, was that cowboy life was dull and, as many critics wrote, Andy Adams was simply too true to be good. Adams's premise was that the cowboy deserved the truth, although most writers—and readers—did not share his concern.

The mass market for popular cowboy writing seemed insatiable. Max Brand, actually one Frederick Faust, earned the title of "King of the Pulps" for producing 179 books containing an estimated 25 million words in twenty years of writing. The still popular Zane Grey, a New York dentist, wrote eighty-five books, fifty-four of which were Westerns. Grey's first book was published in 1903, but he did not gain notoriety until 1912, when he published *Riders of the Purple Sage*. In this novel, the hero rescues his love from Mormon treachery and takes her to a hidden canyon where they are surrounded by beauteous and bountiful nature. The book has sold, to this date, at least 1.8 million copies.

FREDERIC REMINGTON

★ ★ ★

Frederic Remington was the first major American painter to de-emphasize the elemental grandeur of nature and to stress the human presence needed to counteract its grimness. He was also the chief exponent of the rugged Western individualist in visual art.

Born in Canton, New York, in 1861, Remington was the son of a newspaper industrialist. He was sent to military school, where he was quite rebellious. When he was a teenager, he was given an autograph album for his birthday. He lettered on its cover, "Fine Art—Not Autographs," and promptly filled its pages with pen and ink sketches. A description of himself at the age of sixteen was: "My hair is short and stiff and I am about 5 feet 8 [170 cm] and weigh 180 pounds [81 kg]. There is nothing poetical about me." While young Remington had no desire to make art his livelihood, he was, in 1879, one of only two students in the first class of Yale University's School of Art. His mother wanted him to become an industrialist in the manner of a Rockefeller or Carnegie; however, after half a dozen jobs in less than two years, he fell sick, and although he became relatively

healthy, he abhorred industrialized society his entire life. Before setting out for Montana in the early 1880s, Remington became a proficient rifleman and skilled horseman.

In Montana he soon discovered the West to be his natural element. He purchased a 320-acre (128-ha) Kansas ranch, sight unseen; how-

Left: Frederic Remington was the first major American painter to stress the human struggle against the harsh landscape of the West. Below: Remington's Old Time Plains Fight. *Remington's epitaph reads,* HE KNEW THE HORSE.

ever, in 1885 he returned to New York, suffering from ill health and financial disaster. During the army's campaign against Geronimo, Remington was asked to illustrate articles about the campaign; he soon became New York's resident Westerner, drawing for *Harper's*, *Century*, and *Outing*. During this time Theodore Roosevelt became enamoured with Remington's drawing and asked him to illustrate his book, *Ranch Life and the Hunting Trail*. From that point on, Remington never suffered for lack of profit from his artwork and was even said to set fire to piles of his canvases during the later stages of his life out of some perverse sense of pleasure.

It has been said that Remington (along with his friend Teddy Roosevelt) was a misogynist and a racist. Among the hundreds of subjects in his paintings, no more than four women ever appeared in his known Western work. He treated the Indian in his work as if he were part

Below: This photograph of Remington at the age of forty-eight was taken in 1900, shortly before his death. Because he was known to have destroyed some of his work, it is uncertain how much is in existence. It is estimated that Remington completed more than 2,700 paintings. Opposite: Remington's The Snow Trail.

of the hostile environment. He believed that masculine strength came from conflicts with nature. For example, in his *Friend or Foe*, the lone rider is seen straining his eyes, attempting to identify a small apparition on a bleak horizon. In his paintings of lonely cowboys staring out over an unforgiving and hostile nature, and of cavalrymen riding to the attack, Remington depicted a culture triumphant over nature—the white male dominating his lesser environment. Nevertheless, for what they are, and for those they represent, Remington's drawings and paintings are full of spirit, for he did obviously

know from firsthand experience the prairies and the mountains that he so accurately captured on his canvases. One of his outstanding achievements are his illustrations for Francis Parkman's *The Oregon Trail*. Remington even tried his hand at writing a love story, but did not have enough understanding of his female character to complete more than one tale.

Toward the end of his life, Remington began to drink heavily and grow overly fond of food; in fact, he gained so much weight that he was too large to ride a horse (though he did create the first bronze range horse statue, *The Bronco Buster*). Before he died at forty-eight on Christmas Day, 1909, he decided what his epitaph would be: HE KNEW THE HORSE. Although one cannot be sure of the numbers (partially because he destroyed many of his own canvases), it is believed that Frederic Remington completed more than twenty-seven hundred paintings and drawings, illustrated 142 books, and furnished illustrations for forty-one different magazines. In the end, it can be said that he was one of the creators of the Wild West mystique by, as he himself said, making "pictures for boys, for boys from 10 to 70."

CHARLES M. RUSSELL

★ ★ ★

Charles M. Russell was another famous cowboy artist. Humorist Will Rogers wrote the following words about him:

He wasn't just another artist. He wasn't just "another anything." In nothing that he ever did was he "just another." He was a good philosopher: He was a great humorist. He had a great underlying spiritual feeling, and the ordinary customs and habits that are supposed to mark what the well-dressed Christian is wearing this season, but a great sympathy and understanding for the man of the world, be he Indian or white. He didn't think a paved street made a better view. In people he loved human nature. In stories loved human interest. He not only left us great living pictures of what our west was, but he lefts an example of how to live in friendship with all mankind.

Charles Marion Russell was born in 1864 in St. Louis, Missouri. Charles Russell, like Frederic Remington, was born into a wealthy family and, like Remington, was a headstrong boy with a dislike of academics. He had been enrolled in the Burlington Military Academy, but quit and was sent to a local art school of which he would later say, "Hell, they just tried to teach me to draw a straight line." He soon escaped to the great outdoors, where he would find his calling. At the age of sixteen, after devouring countless dime novels about the West, Russell left St. Louis and ended up in Montana, which he would love his entire life. For eleven years he worked as a horse wrangler; during this time, he began to draw and paint his surroundings as well. After marrying, he and his wife settled down in comfort in Great Falls, Montana, where she managed the sale of his work.

Unlike Remington, Russell saw the West as a symbol of complete freedom. He sympathized with outlaws and believed in the basic humanity of the Indian, something that was quite rare in those days. In fact, sometimes Russell tried in his work to capture, almost humorously, the Indian viewpoint in paintings such as his *Indians Discover Lewis and Clark*. (In this painting, the Indians seem both bewildered and amused at the antics of Lewis and Clark, who appear lost and out of place.) Charles Russell painted a boyish and simple West. The lasting popularity of his work illustrates the extent to which most people understood that his art conveyed a love for the freedom, individualism, and simplicity that was associated with the American West.

Right: Russell's The War Party. *Opposite, top: Russell's* Bronc to Breakfast, *1908, watercolor. Opposite, bottom: Russell's* Laugh Kills Lonesome, *c. 1925, oil on canvas.*

CHAPTER 6

SOCIAL

COMMENTATORS

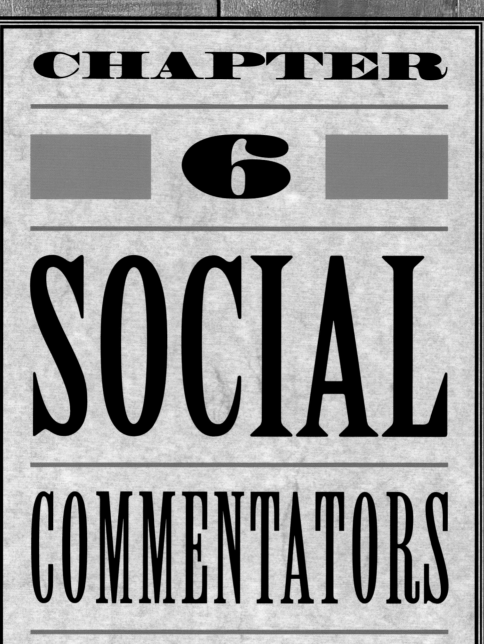

...THE MEN OF THE ALAMO CALL OUT ENCOURAGEMENT TO EACH OTHER; A SETTLER PUSHES WEST AND SINGS HIS SONG, AND THE SONG ECHOES OUT FOREVER AND FILLS THE UNKNOWING AIR.

IT IS THE AMERICAN SOUND: IT IS HOPEFUL, BIG HEARTED, IDEALISTIC--DARING, DECENT AND FAIR. THAT'S OUR HERITAGE, THAT'S OUR SONG. WE SING IT STILL. FOR ALL OUR PROBLEMS, OUR DIFFERENCES, WE ARE TOGETHER AS OF OLD.

---RONALD REAGAN, FROM HIS 1985 INAUGURAL ADDRESS

THE FRIENDLY AND FLOWING SAVAGE, WHO IS HE?
IS HE WAITING FOR CIVILIZATION, OR PAST IT AND MASTERING IT?

---WALT WHITMAN, *SONG OF MYSELF*

The cast of characters who have shaped the West are numerous and diverse. As the Wild West unfolded, many people wrestled with various, often conflicting, visions of the United States. Americans' early ideas about their country and its expansion (often referred to as manifest destiny) include two different if often mingled concepts. On one hand, there was the idea that manifest destiny meant that settlers had the right to build a new social order while excluding those who lived on the land before them. On the other hand, there was the idea that a new order was more of an evolutionary process, whereby society progressed yet incorporated and preserved the old. To this day, this battle rages on. While many, particularly historians and artists, often attempt to uncover the truth in our past, there are those, often politicians, who attempt to cover the past and present with myth in order to preserve what they consider to be the proper American image. Nevertheless, the processes of Western development move forward, from the discovery of untainted land to cattle raising and farming; from farming to hydroelectric power, to preservation and conservation, and, eventually, into space, the newest frontier.

The following are several men whose work was greatly influential in shaping the ideology of the West as well as contributing to its development and preservation. In doing so, they left behind an enduring legacy.

WALT WHITMAN

Walt Whitman is considered by many to be the poet whose work gave the ultimate expression to the idea of manifest destiny. Although Whitman was born in New York State in 1819 and resided his entire life on the Atlantic seaboard (he made an extended trip to New Orleans, and to the West Coast late in his life), he was attracted to the Western intellectual tradition.

The son of a Long Island farmer who became a carpenter and moved his family to Brooklyn, New York, in 1823, Whitman left school at the age of eleven. He worked as an office boy and later for a doctor. From an early age he was fascinated with the novels of Sir Walter Scott and by the age of twelve, he began working for a newspaper and contributing articles. By the time he was fifteen, after his family relocated into the interior of Long Island, the young Whitman was completely on his own. During the next six years he began to write poetry in earnest and taught school. By the 1840s he began to link America's territorial acquisition to personal and civic betterment and became a Free-soiler, one who was opposed to the addition of more slave territories. In 1855 he published his opus, *Leaves of Grass*, which included an engraving opposite its title page that demonstrated Whitman's belief in the connection between geographical and personal expansion. The engraving was of a bearded, working man at rest. He wore a broad hat, and his shirt was open at the neck, revealing a colored undershirt; his right arm was akimbo and his left hand was hidden in his pants pocket. In the preface, Whitman wrote that the poet of America "incarnates its geography and natural life and rivers and lakes."

In the 1860 edition of *Leaves of Grass* Whitman wrote, "These States tend inland, and toward the Western sea, and I will also," making up his mind that his audience of the future would be from the western territories. He rejoiced in America's huge prairies, Great Plains, and Rocky Mountains. He also became immersed in the idea of a fated course of empire building that led Americans to the shores of the Pacific.

"Pioneers! O Pioneers," is probably Whitman's most ebullient poem about westward movement, as it charts the march of the pioneer hordes who, unlike the weakening peoples of the Old World, are youthful and strong, and shoulder a cosmic burden. He wrote: "This army of pioneers conquers the wilderness and

the mountains and arrives at the Pacific Ocean to embark on a newer and mightier world. . . ."

Whitman saw the move westward as a restoration of humankind's lost harmony with nature. He believed that the conquering of the West would lead America into a fuller understanding of itself and nature, welding both into a permanent kind of communion. As he wrote in "Passage to India":

All these hearts, as of fretted children, shall be
*   sooth'd,*
All affection shall be fully responded to—the secret
*   shall be told;*
All these separations and gaps shall be taken up,
*   and hook'd and link'd together;*

The whole earth—this cold, impassive, voiceless
*   Earth, shall be completely justified; . . .*
Nature and man shall be disjoin'd and diffused no
*   more,*
The true Son of God shall absolutely fuse them.

This unquenchable enthusiasm for America and its vast wilderness and seemingly endless possibilities made Walt Whitman a truly inspirational giant not just among poets, but also to those people who viewed the settling of the West as the beginning of harmony—the marriage of humankind.

Whitman died in 1892, secure in the knowledge that he had been faithful to his muse and his dream.

THEODORE ROOSEVELT

★ ★ ★

The world of cattle was male dominated and consequently created a cult of masculine ideals and virtues. While women were often revered and seen as being in need of protection, the cowboys often held their horses in higher esteem. Furthermore, this need for male domination is most probably what has made the cowboy continue to be an American icon. One of the most influential supporters of this way of thinking and living was Theodore Roosevelt, who fell in love with the West and its lure of manliness.

Theodore Roosevelt was born to a wealthy family in New York City in 1858. Roosevelt was a nearsighted and asthmatic youth. By the time he was twenty-five, he felt hemmed in by the pressures of society; shaken by a death in his family, he invested in a cattle ranch, Elk Horn Ranch, in the Dakota Badlands. By mid-1884, he had begun to live in a cabin there and was supervising the building up of a herd of cattle. Soon after, he acquired another ranch, the Maltese Cross, with his partners.

It was in the Dakota Badlands that Roosevelt, with his thin boyish face, his oversized teeth, thick glasses, and New York City demeanor, began to flourish. It is reported that toward the beginning of this period of adjustment he once yelled this formal command to his cowhands: "Hasten forward quickly, there." However, he soon adapted to his environment and was said to be able to stay in the saddle for up to thirteen hours a day overseeing work or riding for pleasure among the sagebrush and the pines on his ranches. Within several months he wrote, "This country is growing on me more and more; it has a curious, fantastic beauty all its own." He also gained thirty pounds (13.5 kg) and the weathered look of a cowboy.

Also during this period, Roosevelt began to view the saddle and the rifle as an inseparable pair. As he killed a succession of larger and larger animals his joy grew into excitement. When he finally killed two grizzly bears (one felled at a great distance with two shots, the other dropped with one shell from eight paces away), his companions said that they remembered the woods echoing with his happiness. Later, upon returning to the East, Roosevelt brought huge crates of stuffed animal heads, most of which accompanied him to the White House. Roosevelt would later write that "The hunter is the archetype of freedom," and he often described his hunting companions as "fearless and reckless."

It is no wonder then that Roosevelt saw that the cowboy embodied everything good: fearlessness, recklessness, independence, boldness, and masculinity. To this man, straight shooting was American, and violence was the norm. Consequently, the West sym-

Below: President Theodore Roosevelt poised and ready to enter Yellowstone National Park. Opposite: Theodore Roosevelt in his beloved natural habitat. He held the belief that "The hunter is the archetype of freedom."

bolized the best of America; he believed that if the East would imitate the West it could be redeemed from its ensuing softness. The joy of the fight carried him and his cowboy regiment, the Rough Riders, up San Juan Hill in southeast Cuba into victory during the Spanish-American War, and he gloried in "the victory and the gore."

Later, prior to becoming president of the United States, he often engaged in athletic competition with his friends and colleagues. Gifford Pinchot, head of the Department of Agriculture's Division of Forestry wrote, "T.R. and I did a little wrestling, at which he beat me; and some boxing, during which I had the honor of knocking the future President of the United States off his very solid pins." After he became

Roosevelt loved to ride and to take in the grandeur of the great outdoors.

president, Roosevelt would take long walks in the winter. One such November walk is remembered by Pinchot during which the stroll eventually led them to swim a river. When Pinchot reached home, still wet from the swim, his servant commented, "You've been with the President again."

This active aggression is what possibly led Roosevelt to eschew peace as weakness, and to extoll might, firmness, vigor, and power as masculine and natural. He was close friends with Frederic Remington, and both men believed masculinity to be a prerequisite for success and survival. Etched into the national mind, this thinking is still a part of the American heritage, a cowboy concept in full masculine array.

JOHN WESLEY POWELL

★ ★ ★

John Wesley Powell, born in 1834, was the son of an itinerant Methodist preacher. Although he nearly became a preacher like his father, by the time Powell entered Oberlin College in Illinois, his love of science had won over religion. There he became president of the Illinois Natural History Society and began to embark upon his passionate career as a geologist and explorer. Powell's heroic contribution to America's West may not be as grand as some of the other people mentioned here, but his is certainly more long-lasting and environmentally sound. Powell was one of the first proponents for the preservation of natural habitats. Also, through Congress and legislation, Powell attempted to slow down the rapid onslaught of settlers to the West and to formulate a plan that would protect the land that so many depended upon for their livelihood.

A Civil War veteran, Powell lost a forearm after the Battle of Shiloh. He was unhindered by his handicap and began teaching geology at Oberlin and escorted small groups of students on treks to the Rocky Mountains and across the Great Plains. In 1869, backed by the Smithsonian Institution, he led an expedition from Illinois to the Colorado River and then used the river to cross through the Grand Canyon. In 1871, he made the expedition again.

From 1880 to 1894, Powell served as the director of the United States Geological Survey. It was during these years that his scientific knowledge, expertise, and leadership qualities attracted national attention.

In 1877, in his *Report on the Lands of the Arid Region of the United States,* Powell argued that laws and men must be linked with the environment—a concept that did not quite sit well with those who sought to keep expanding west. He suggested that using the then-ideal land unit of the East, 640 acres (256 ha), of which 160 (64 ha), or one-fourth, was the basic size of a farm which would be sufficient in most eastern areas for keeping a family well off, was

not applicable to the West, which had large arid plains and vast deserts. He knew that land without water was of no use and therefore made careful calculations, calling upon farmers and the government to use irrigation to reduce the basic Western farm size to eighty acres (32 ha), which would still allow farmers to prosper similarly. If the land was not irrigated and was used to run cattle, 2,560 acres (1,024 ha) would be needed to make the farm successful. Powell fought against the English principle of riparian rights (transported from the East to the West), which stated that he who owned the banks of the stream was entitled to all the water there, while others who lived farther away from the stream got none. This early concern for the protection of pure water for the many and not the few was a bold proposition.

John W. Powell was one of the first protectionists in the United States. He fought hard for pure water and the preservation of nature.

The first camp of John Powell. This photograph was taken at Green River Wyoming, in 1871

Powell's dream, however, was in direct antithesis to America's dream of expansion: only today do we look upon such a concept as forward thinking and revolutionary. In 1878–1879, when Powell's program was brought to the floor of the House of Representatives, in opposition to the popular Homestead Act, it was attacked and defeated, and was seen as an attempt to close off the development of the West. Powell had made a serious error. He had demanded that the West submit to a rational and scientific revision of its core belief, manifest destiny. This dream, flying in the face of all else at the time, was, to put it simply, heroic.

JOHN MUIR
★ ★ ★

John Muir was a Scottish-born American naturalist, explorer, conservationist, and writer. Born in 1838 and raised in Dunbar, Scotland, near the North Sea, Muir came with his family to America and settled on a Wisconsin farm in 1849. The son of strict Presbyterians, Muir always believed that the intense working of the land (stressed by his father), made him into a "runt" for his entire life. Although his father imposed bedtime after supper, young Muir engineered a series of clockwork weights and pulleys that pulled him straight up in bed at three in the morning so that he might have time to do what he loved—read. By this method, Muir was able to study mathematics and the classics and to enter the University of Wisconsin at Madison. However, he soon tired of academia and left for what he later called, "the university of the wilderness."

For the rest of his life, Muir studied nature in its natural splendor. He traveled extensively throughout the United States, Canada, and Mexico, as well as to Alaska and the South Seas. He spent years camping in Yosemite and filled almost one hundred notebooks with descriptions of lizard tracks, cloud formations, glacial terrain, and bird calls. He grew grapes and cherries for money, and when Ralph Waldo Emerson visited Yosemite with Muir in 1871, Emerson slept indoors, while Muir slept under the stars. Emerson wrote of the experience that the wilderness made a good mistress but an intolerable wife.

Muir became the spokesman for the forests and mountains, much like John Powell spoke for the farmer and the land. Muir believed that humanity's problems could be cured with a return to the wilderness. He saw the destruction of natural beauty as a crime against life, a sin against the harmony that humankind should seek to obtain. Muir was a rugged individualist who grew his hair to his shoulders and never trimmed his beard, but, nevertheless, was savvy enough to carry his message of the need for harmony with nature to Congress and the business community. He rallied against "the hoofed locusts," his name for the sheep that were permitted to overgraze and destroy the natural ground foliage.

It is because of Muir that Yosemite was made a national park in 1890. In 1892 he helped to create the Sierra Club, of which he was president for twenty-two years, which is dedicated to "the support and cooperation of the people and the government in preserving the forests and other natural features of the Sierra Nevada Mountains."

In 1897, John Muir accompanied Gifford Pinchot, head of the Department of Agriculture's Division of Forestry, on a trip to the Grand Canyon and, as Pinchot told it, the only moment of disagreement between the two men came when they were walking and came upon a tarantula. While Pinchot started to kill it, Muir staunchly defended the spider, declaring that it had every right to coexist with them. In 1902, Muir took President Theodore Roosevelt on a camping trip into Yosemite National Park. It is said that Muir chided the president about his passion for game hunting and asked him when he was going to grow out of it. Muir was an extremely persuasive man, and it was often in the course of conversations such as these that Muir opened the door for a great many conservation laws to become enacted from 1901 to 1909. One of these laws, the Newlands Act, passed in 1902, allocated water resources and created irrigation projects. Muir also convinced Roosevelt not only to create four more national parks, Crater Lake, Mesa Verde, Platte, and Wind Cave, but also to protect such areas as the Grand Canyon, the Petrified Forest, and Mount Lassen until they could be made into national parks.

Although the advent of the Taft administration and World War I eroded this progress, the first steps toward such legislation were taken because of Muir, who saw that the issue was not merely conservation but a need for humankind to live in balance with nature, and that a weakening of even one part weakens the whole. Muir began the call for what would one day be viewed as preservation. Although much of his fight was lost in the years that followed, John Muir's work did sound the initial alarm against wasting natural resources. That alone is worth calling him a hero, particularly in light of our environment's present state.

Grand Canyon of the Yellowstone, by Thomas Moran. Paintings such as this one attempt to convey the beauty found in nature in order to create a sense of wonder and awe, perhaps thereby fostering a sense of duty to preserve and protect its magnificence.

BIBLIOGRAPHY

★ ★ ★

The Beadle Collection of Dime Novels. New York: The New York Public Library, 1922.

Drago, Harry S. *The Legend Makers*. New York: Dodd, Mead & Co., 1960.

Fishwick, Marshall W. "The Cowboy: America's Contribution to the World's Mythology." *Western Folklore* 11:2 (April 1952), 77–92.

Folson, James K. *The American Western Novel*. New Haven: Yale University Press, 1966.

Freedman, Russell. *Cowboys of the Wild West*. New York: Clarion Books, 1985.

Jordan, Roy A., and Tim R. Miller. "The Politics of a Cowboy Culture." *Annals of Wyoming* 52:1 (Spring 1980), 40–45.

Lawrence, Elizabeth Atwood. *Rodeo: An Anthropologist Looks at the Wild and the Tame*. Chicago: University of Chicago Press, 1984.

Lenihan, John H. *Showdown: Confronting Modern America in the Western Film*. Urbana, Ill.: University of Chicago Press, 1980.

Milton, John R. *The Novel of the American West*. Lincoln: University of Nebraska Press, 1980.

Rogin, Michael P. *Ronald Reagan, the Movie and Other Episodes in Political Demonology*. Berkeley: University of California Press, 1987.

Siringo, Charles A. *Riata and Sours: The Story of a Lifetime Spent in the Saddle*. Boston: Houghton Mifflin (reprint), 1931.

Slatta, Richard W. *Cowboys of the Americas*. New Haven: Yale University Press, 1990.

Slotkin, Richard. *The Fatal Environment: The Myth of the Frontier in the Age of Industrialization, 1800–1890*. New York: Atheneum, 1985.

Smith, Dwight L., ed. *The American and Canadian West: A Bibliography*. Santa Barbara: ABC-Clio Press, 1979.

Smith, Henry Nash. *Virgin Land: The American West as Symbol and Myth*. Cambridge: Harvard University Press, 1970.

Taylor, Lonn, and Ingrid Maar. *The American Cowboy*. New York: Harper and Row, 1983.

Tinker, Edward Larocque. *The Horsemen of the Americas and the Literature They Inspired*. Rev. ed. Austin: University of Texas Press, 1967.

Webb, Walter Prescott. *The Great Frontier*. Austin: University of Texas Press, 1951.

Whitman, Walt. *Leaves of Grass*. Boston, 1860.

Wright, Robert M. *Dodge City: The Cowboy Capital and the Great Southwest*. Wichita: Beacon Press, 1913.

Utley, Robert M. *Billy the Kid: A Short and Violent Life*. Lincoln and London: University of Nebraska Press, 1989.

INDEX

SOURCES